Doodle Invasion

L'album a colorier

par Zifflin

Illustré par

Kerby Rosanes

Copyright © 2013 Zifflin

All rights reserved.

ISBN: 1494347148
ISBN-13: 978-1494347147

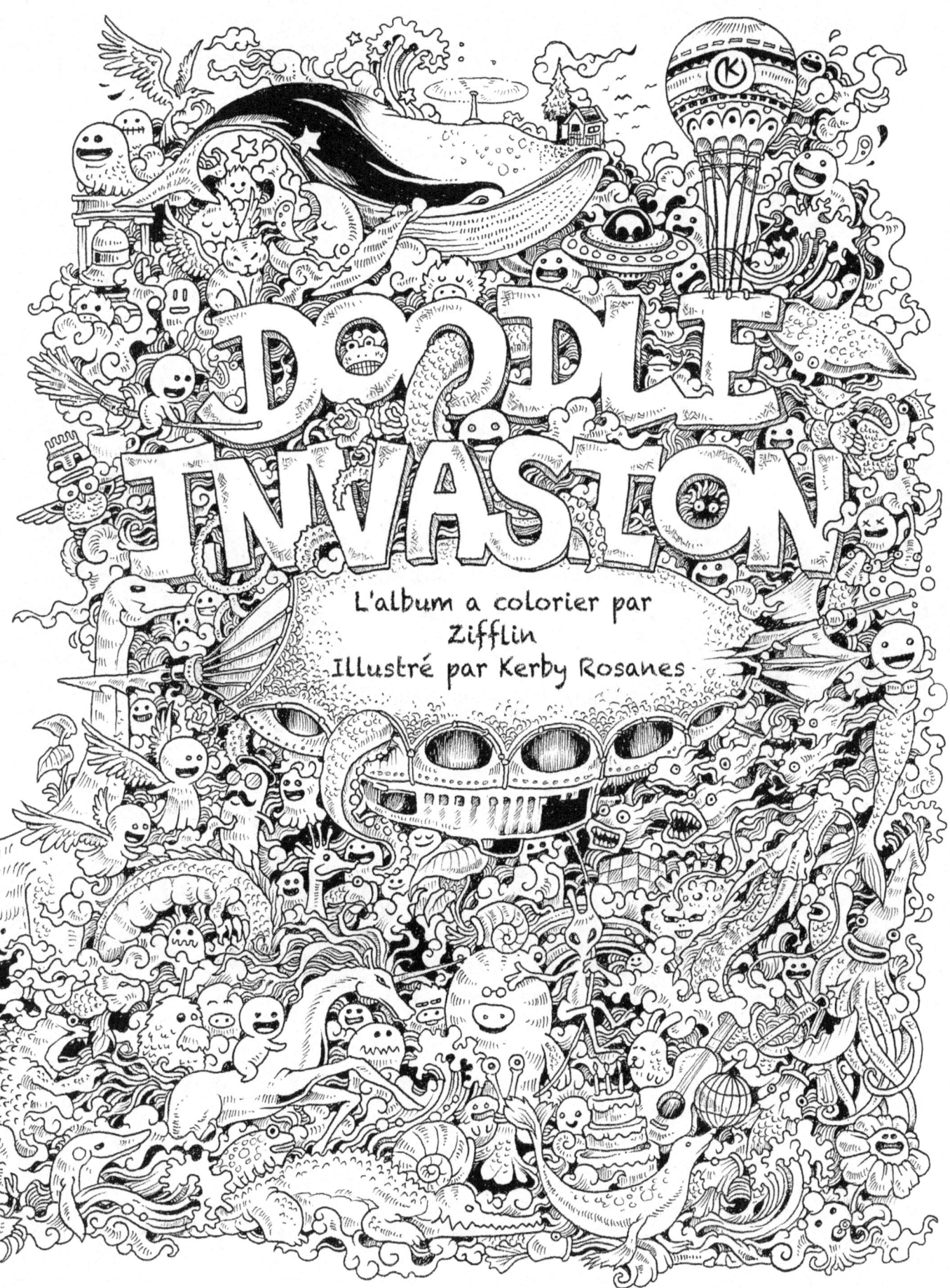

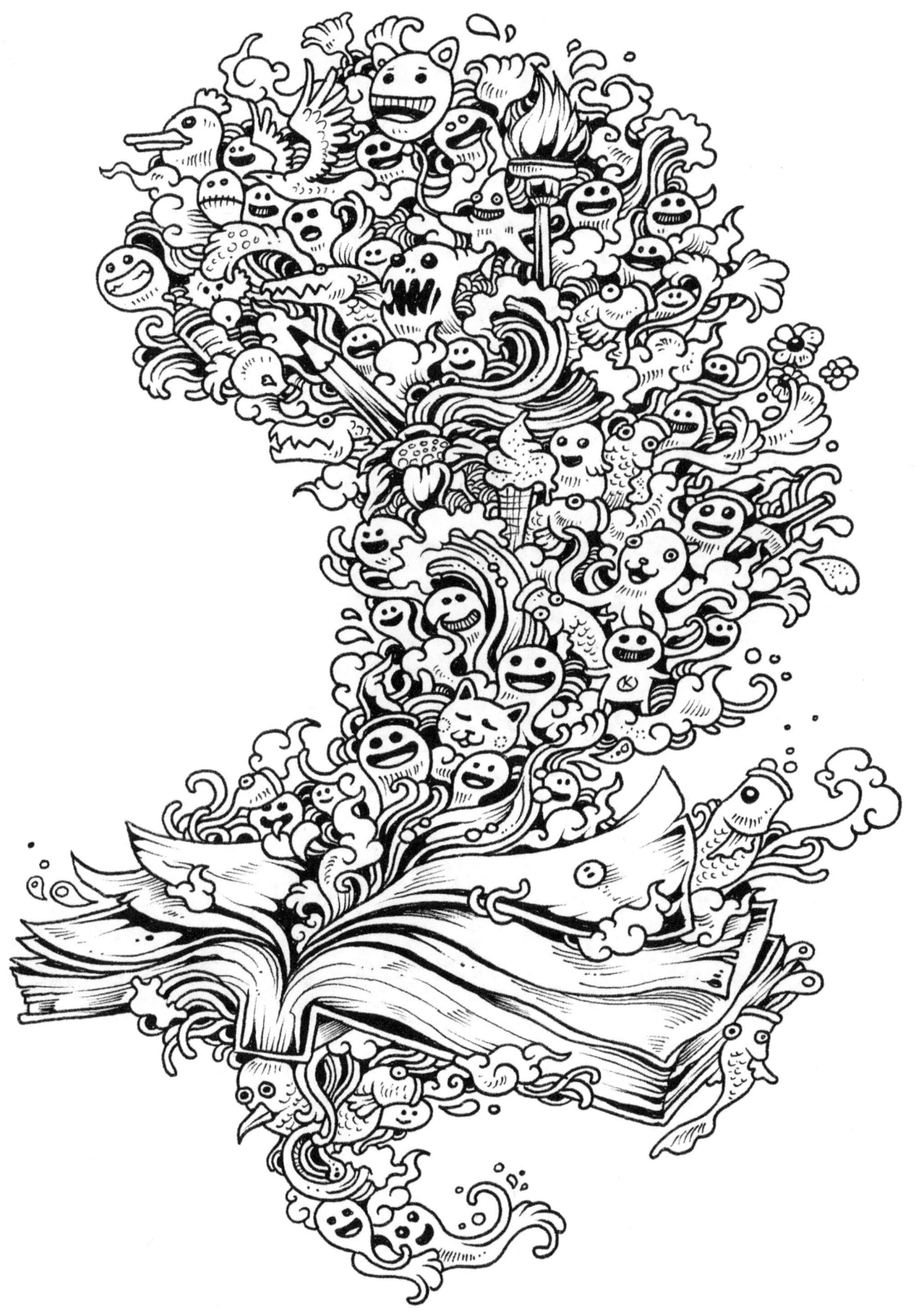

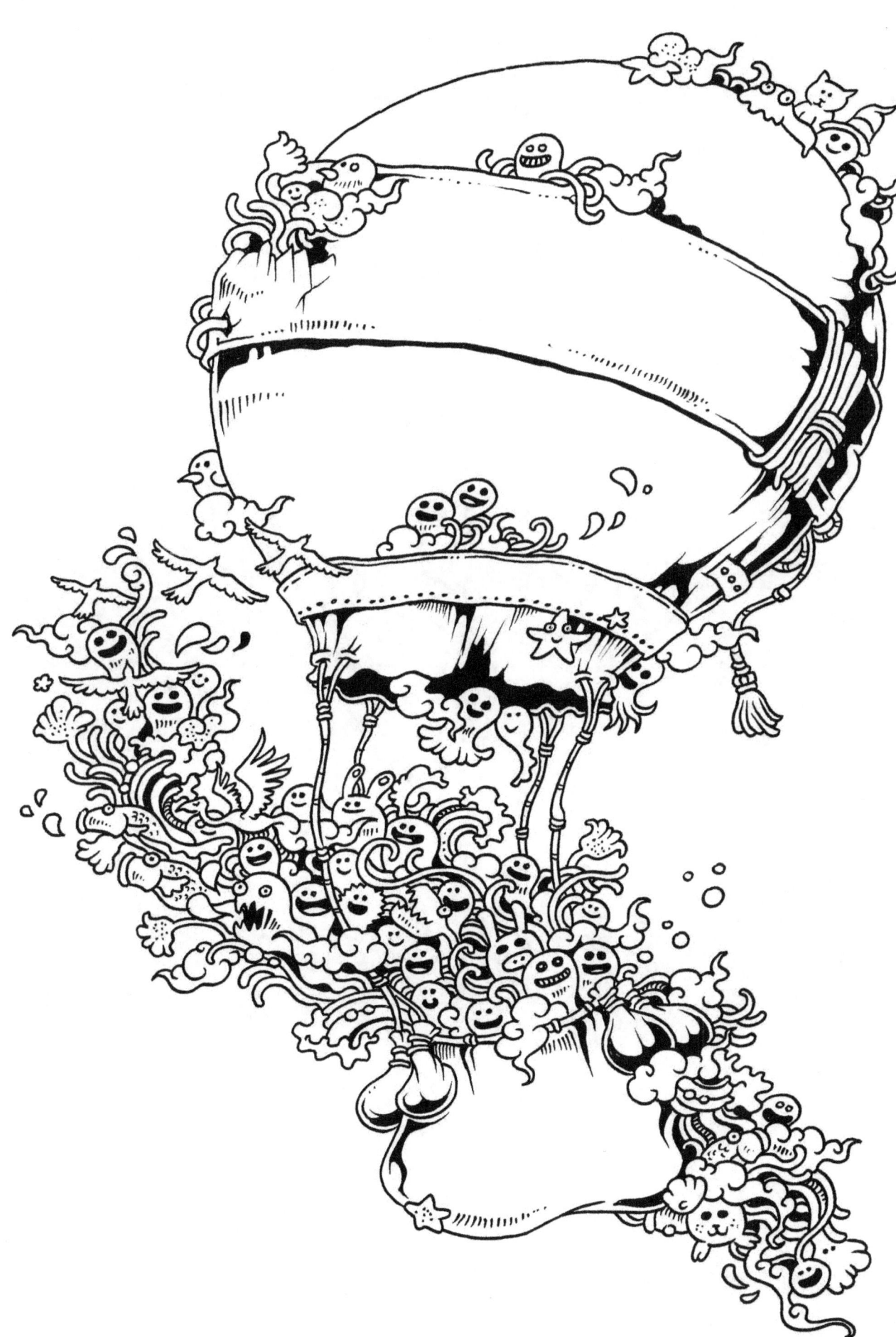

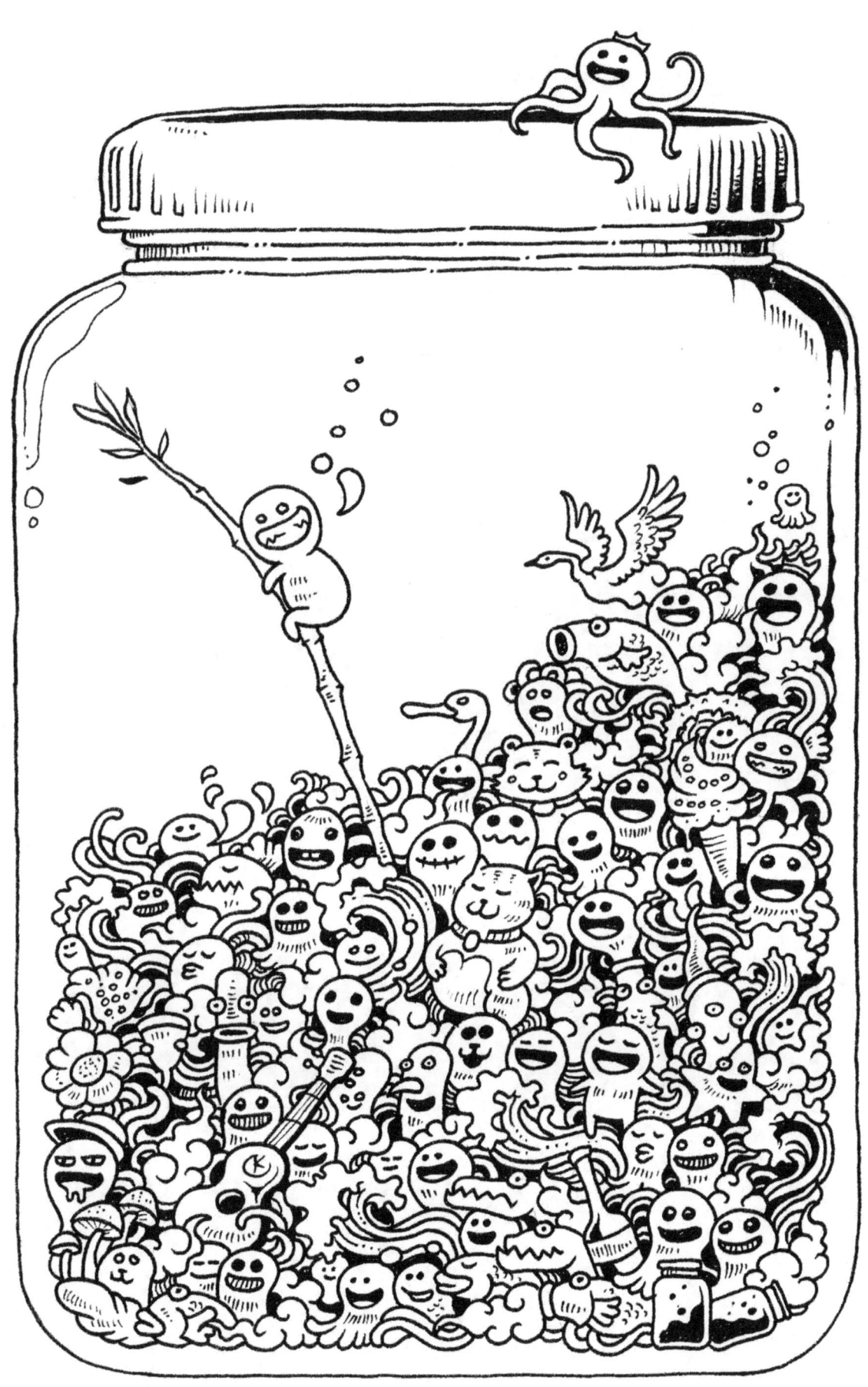

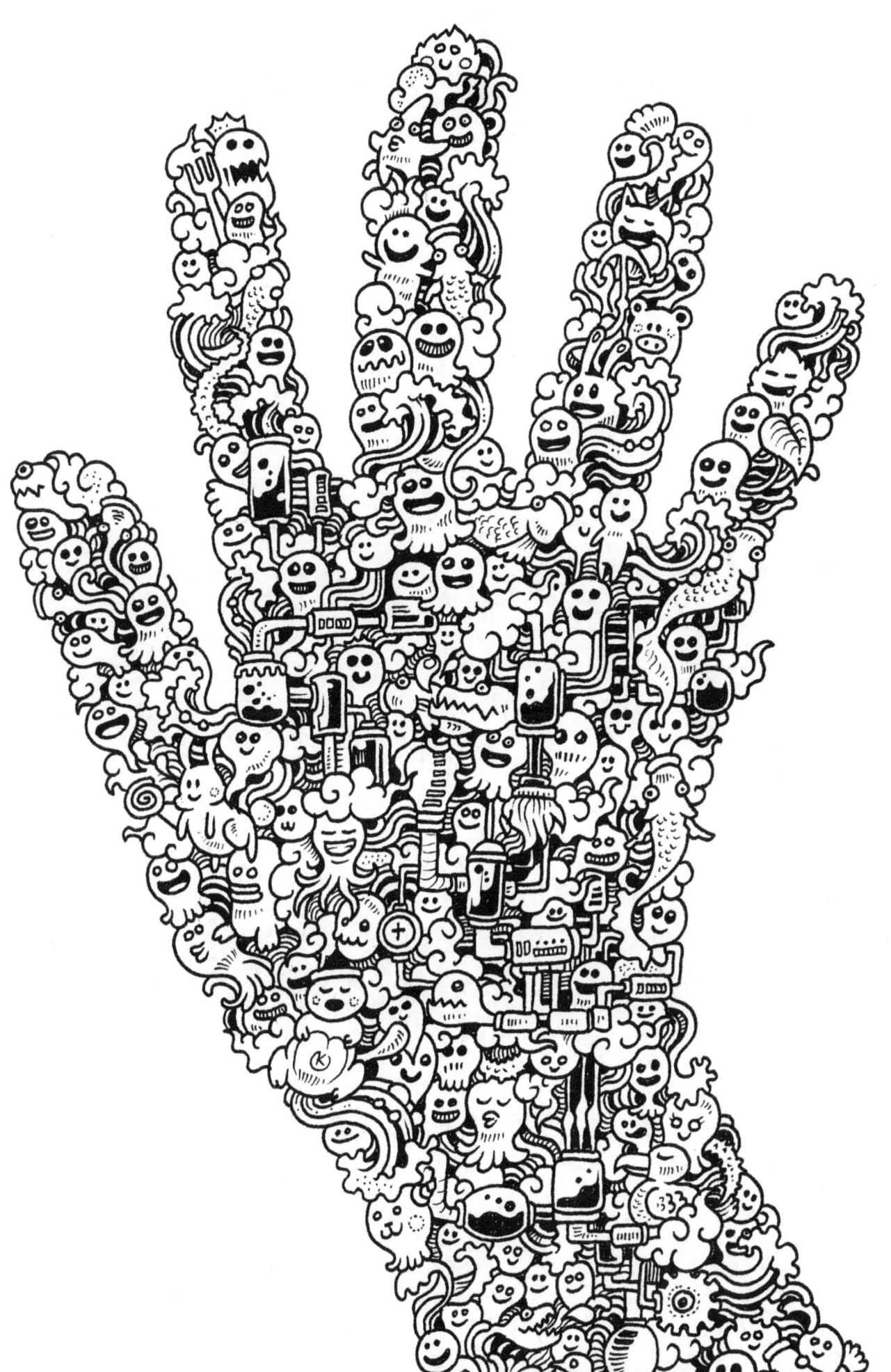

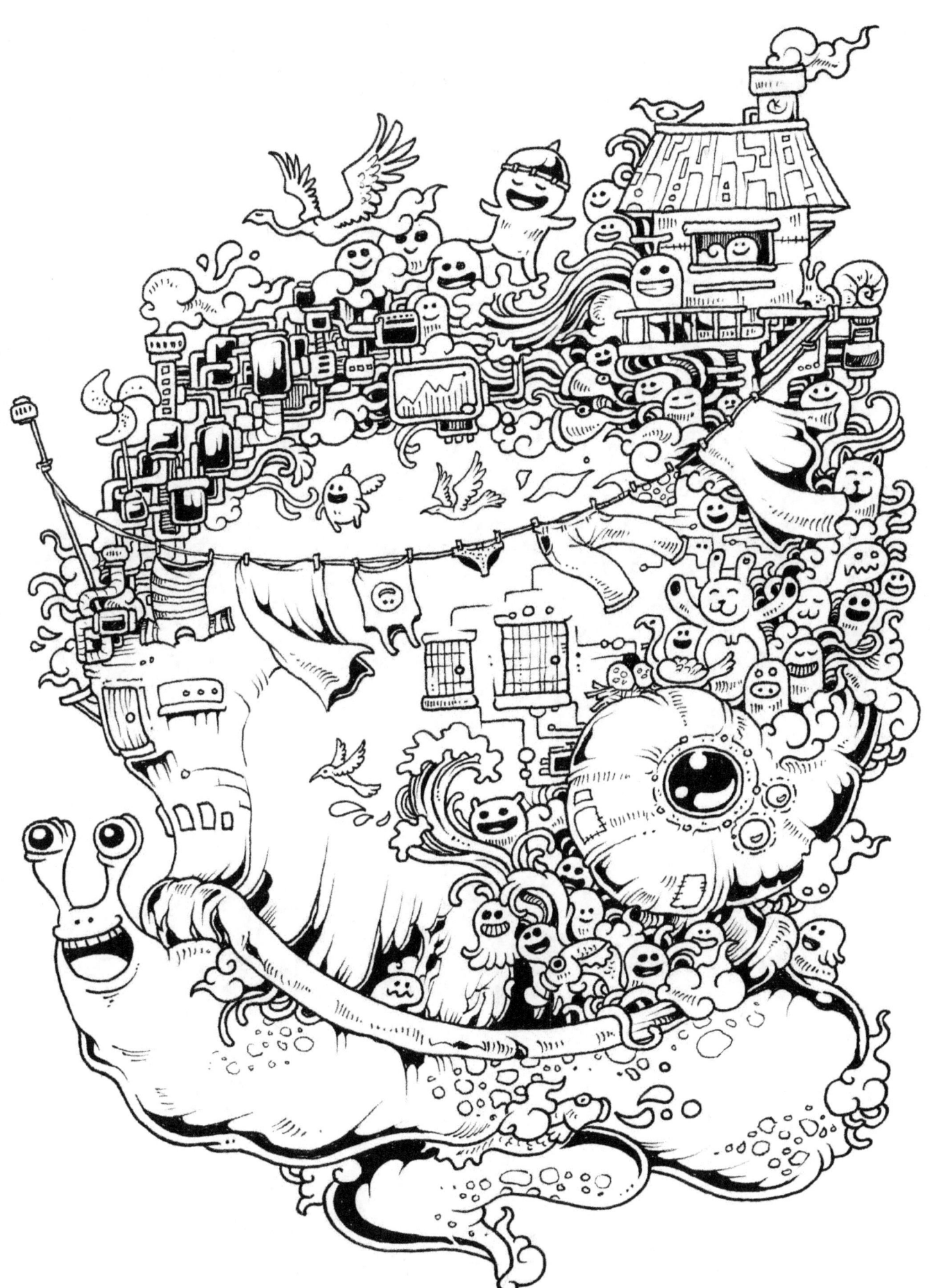

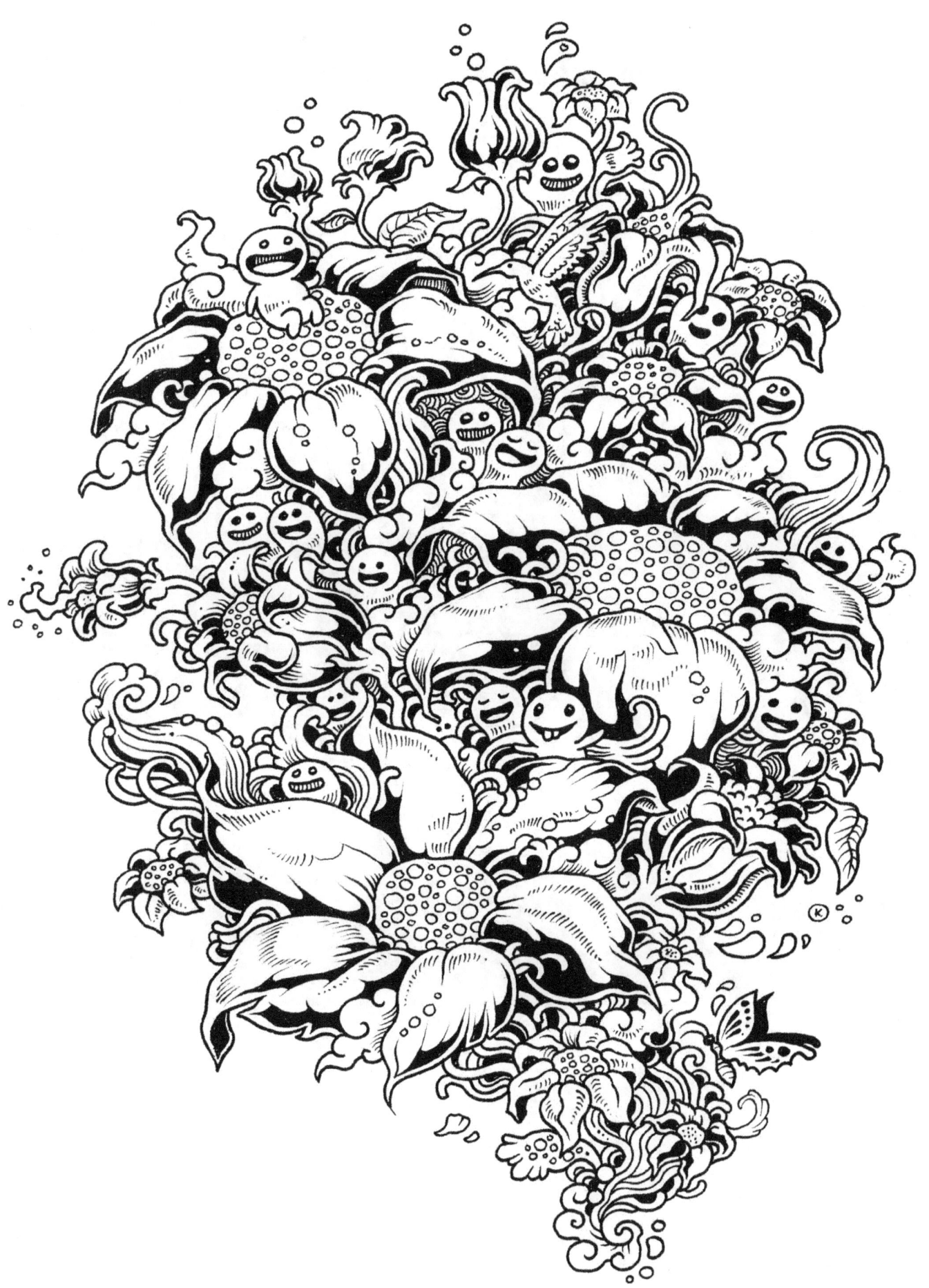

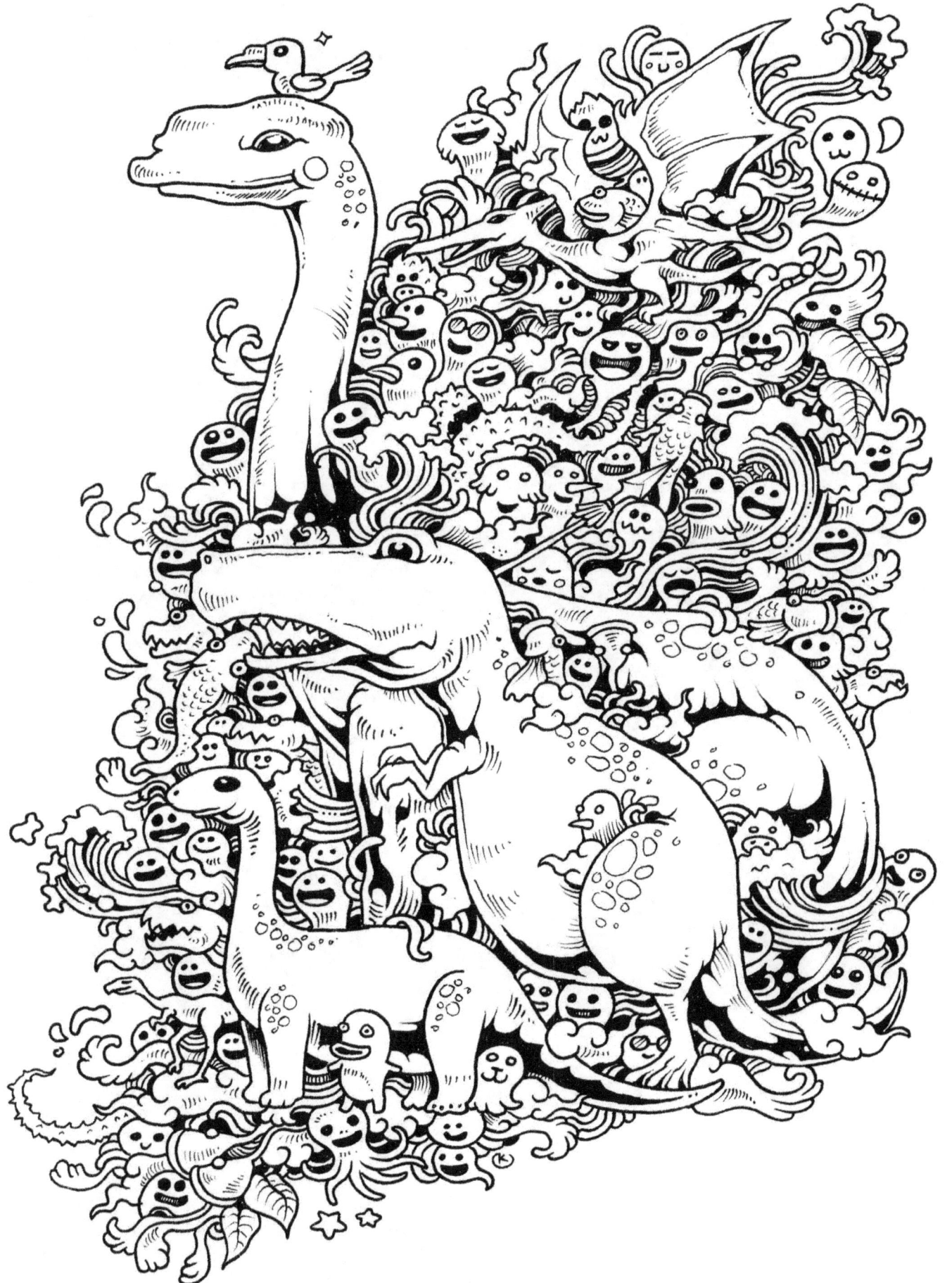

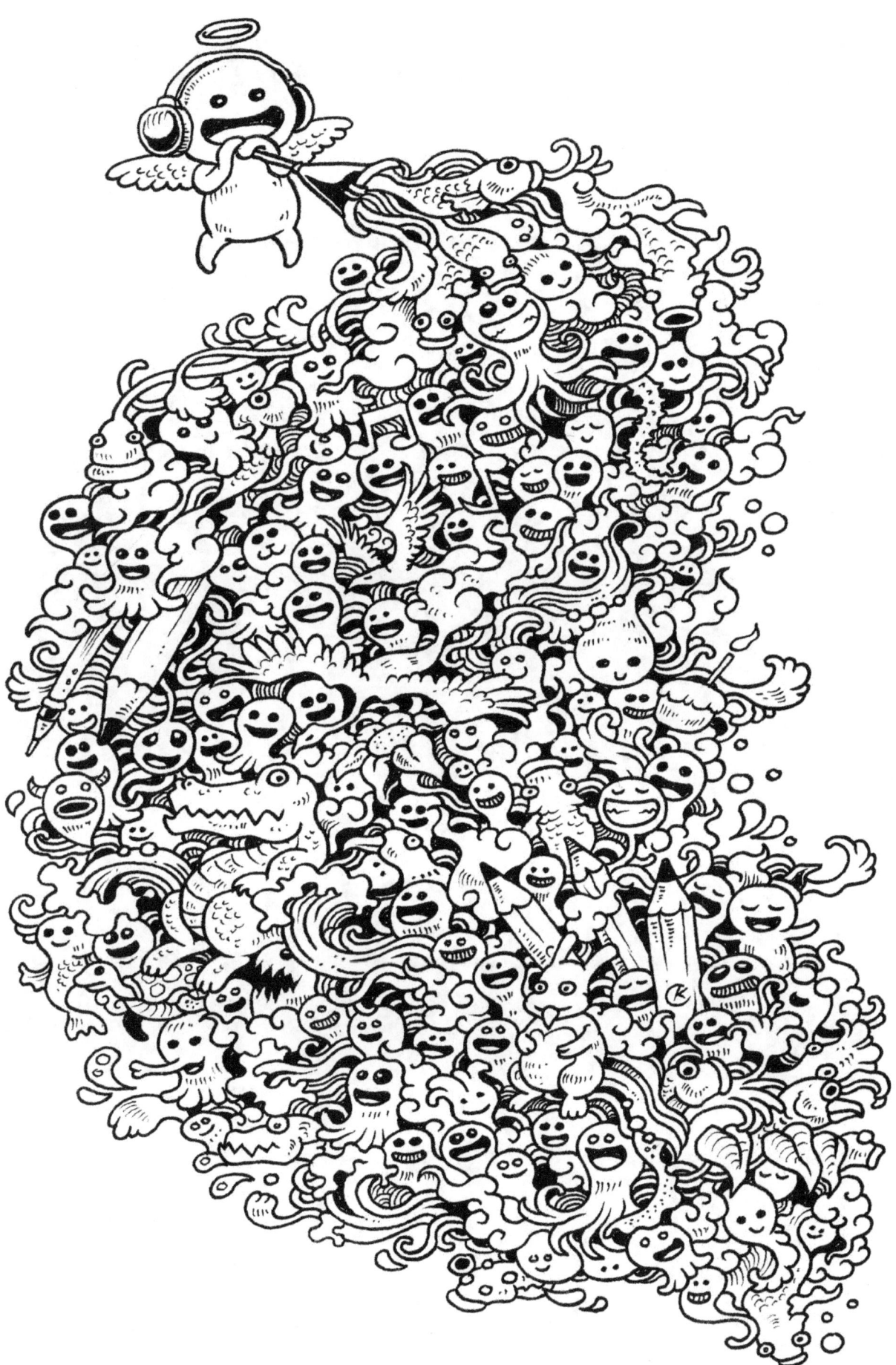

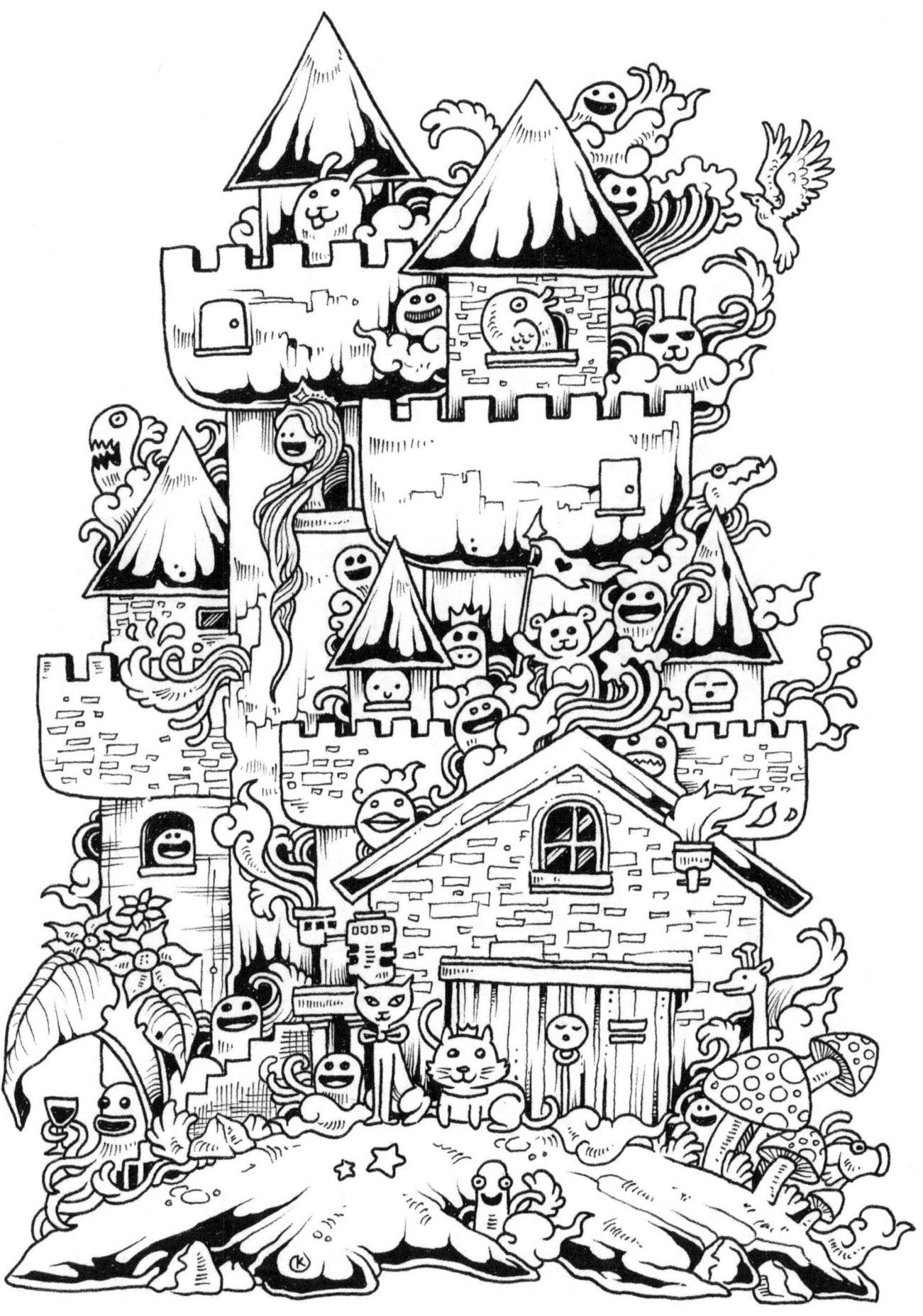

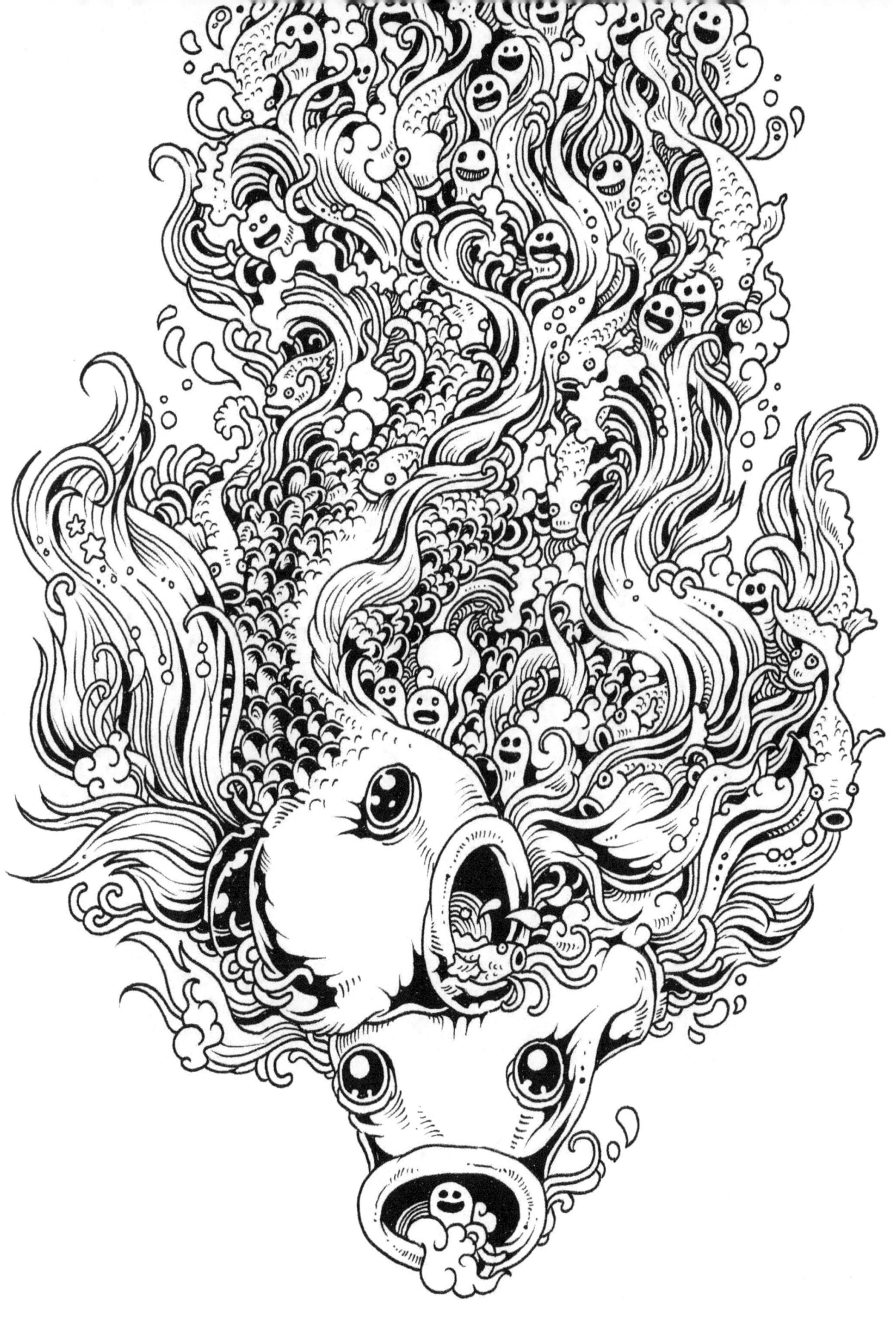

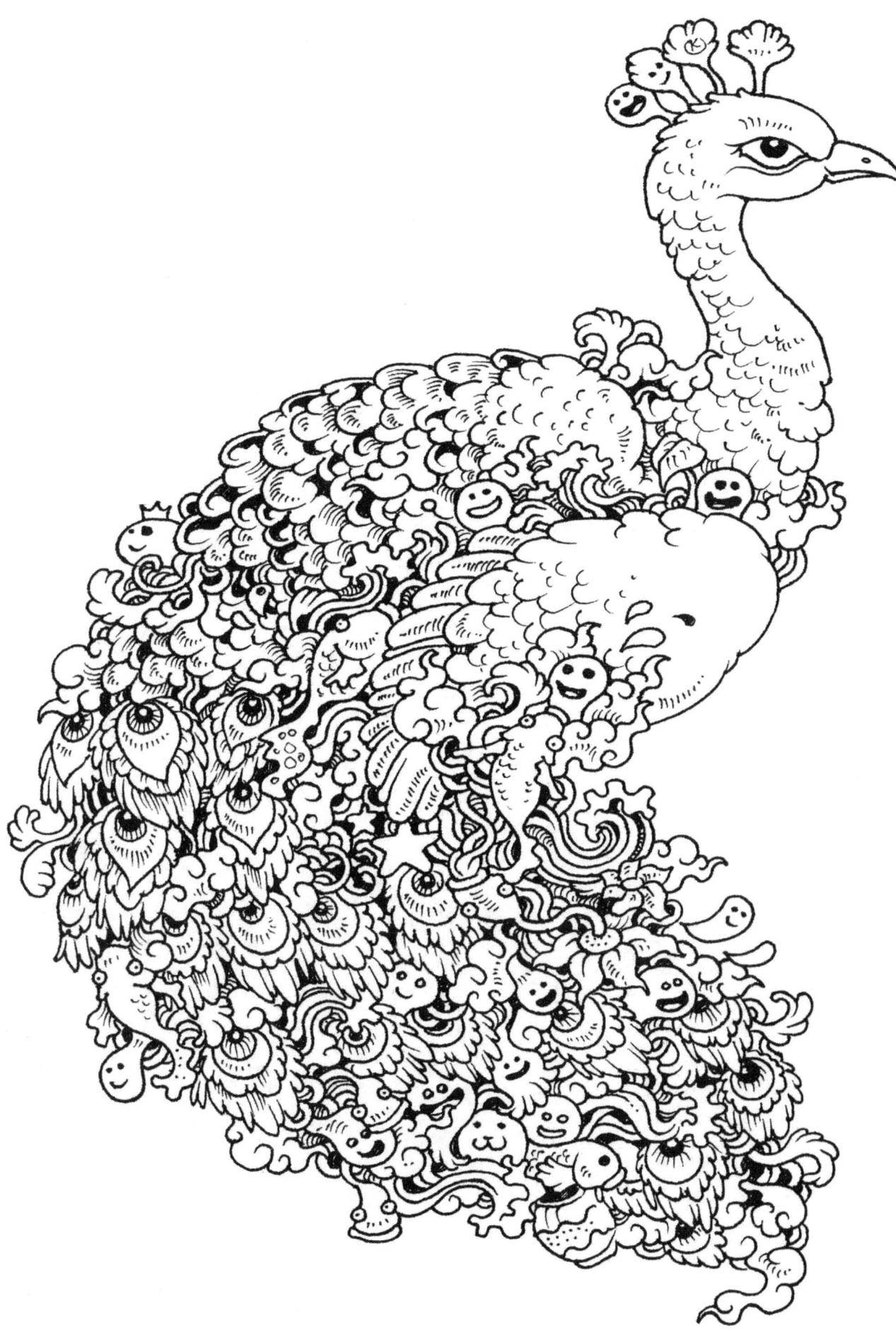

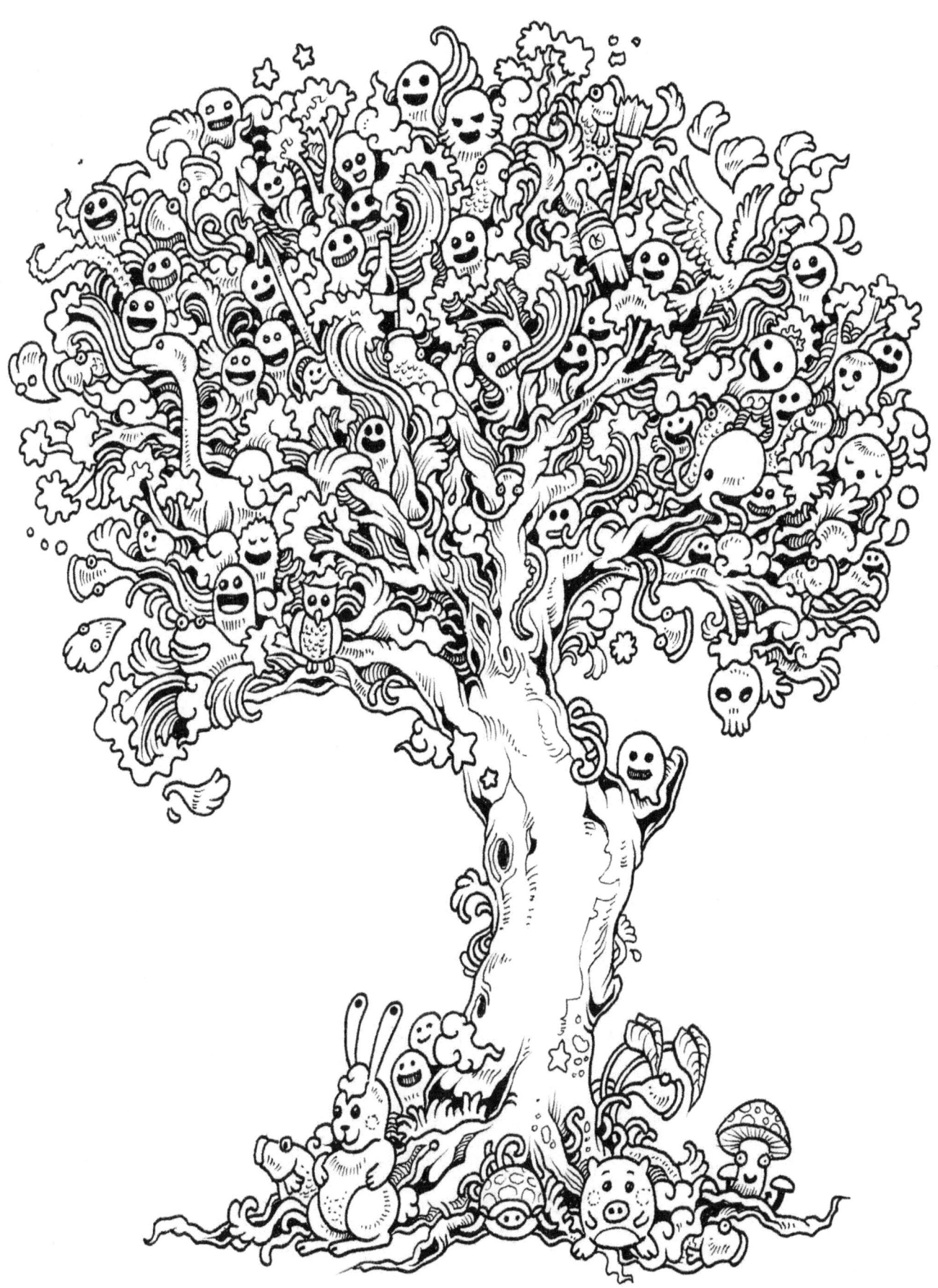

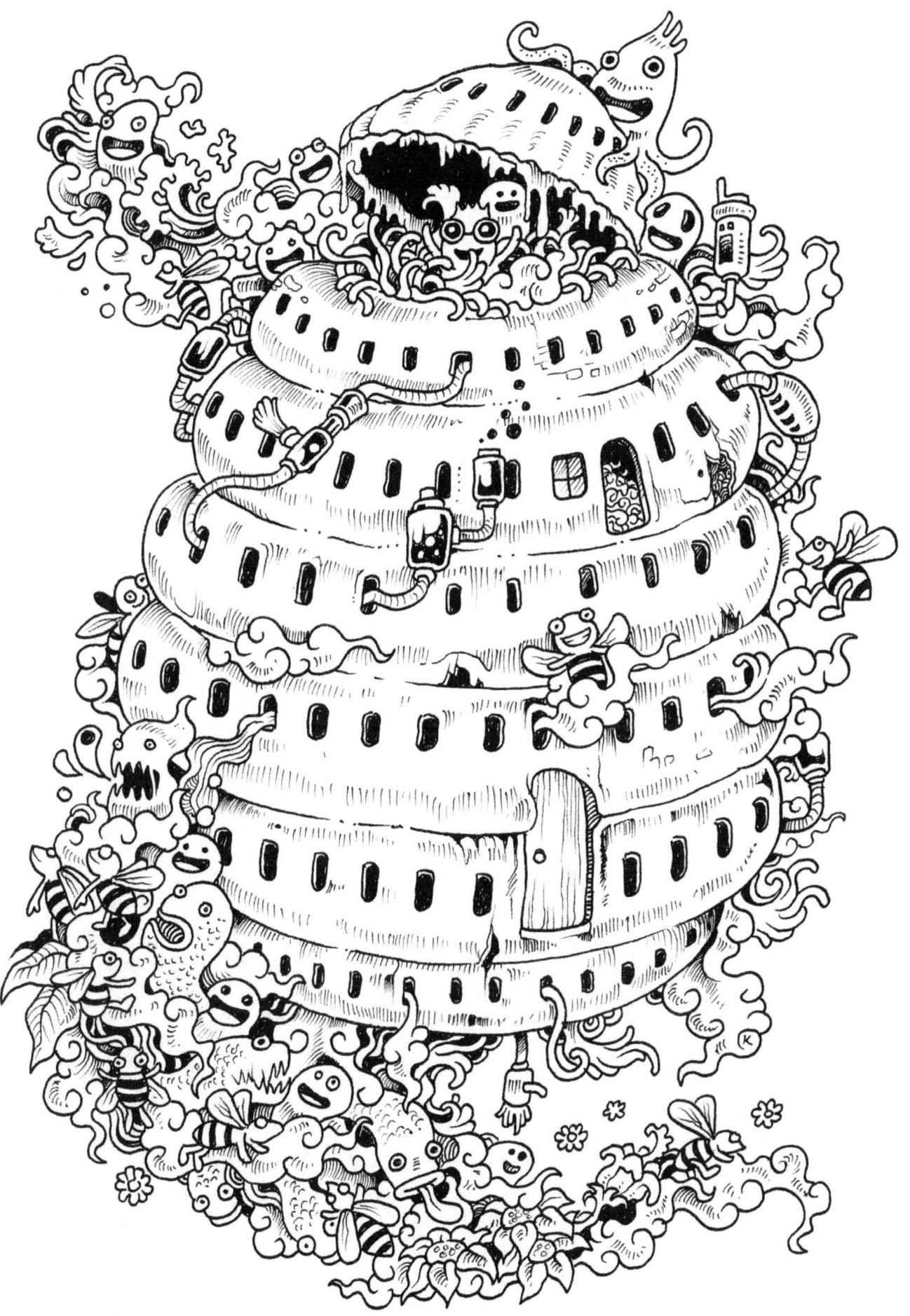

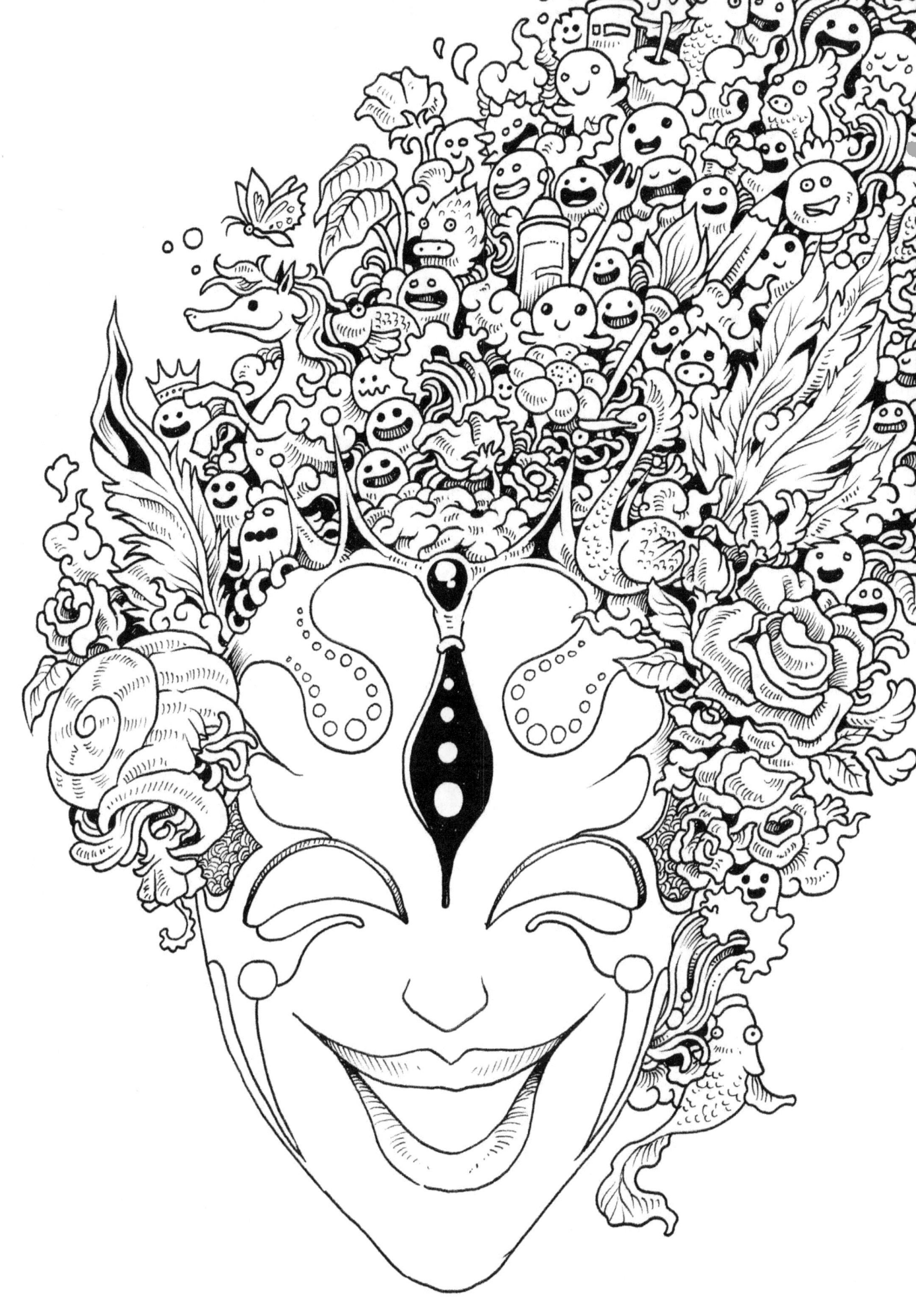

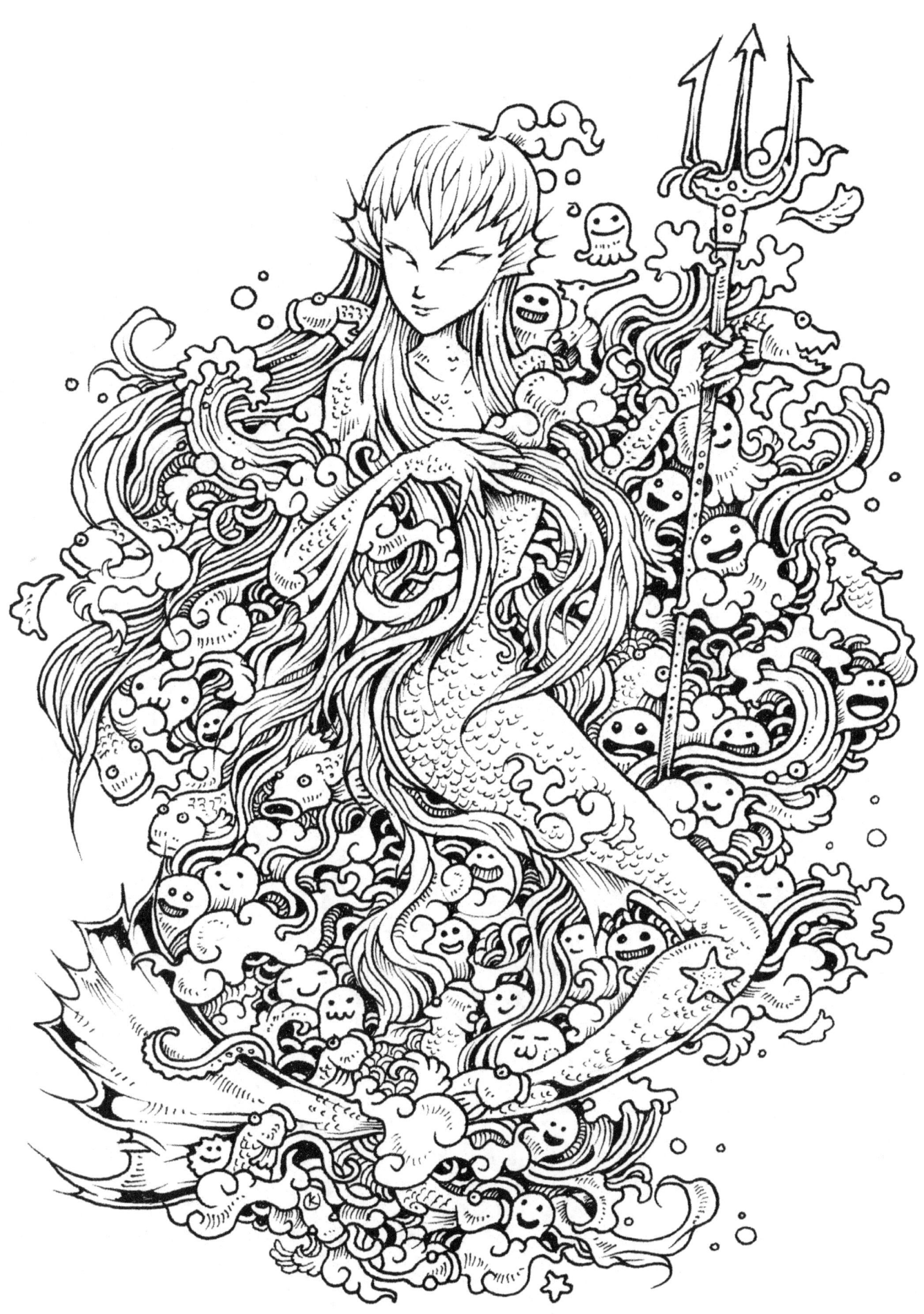

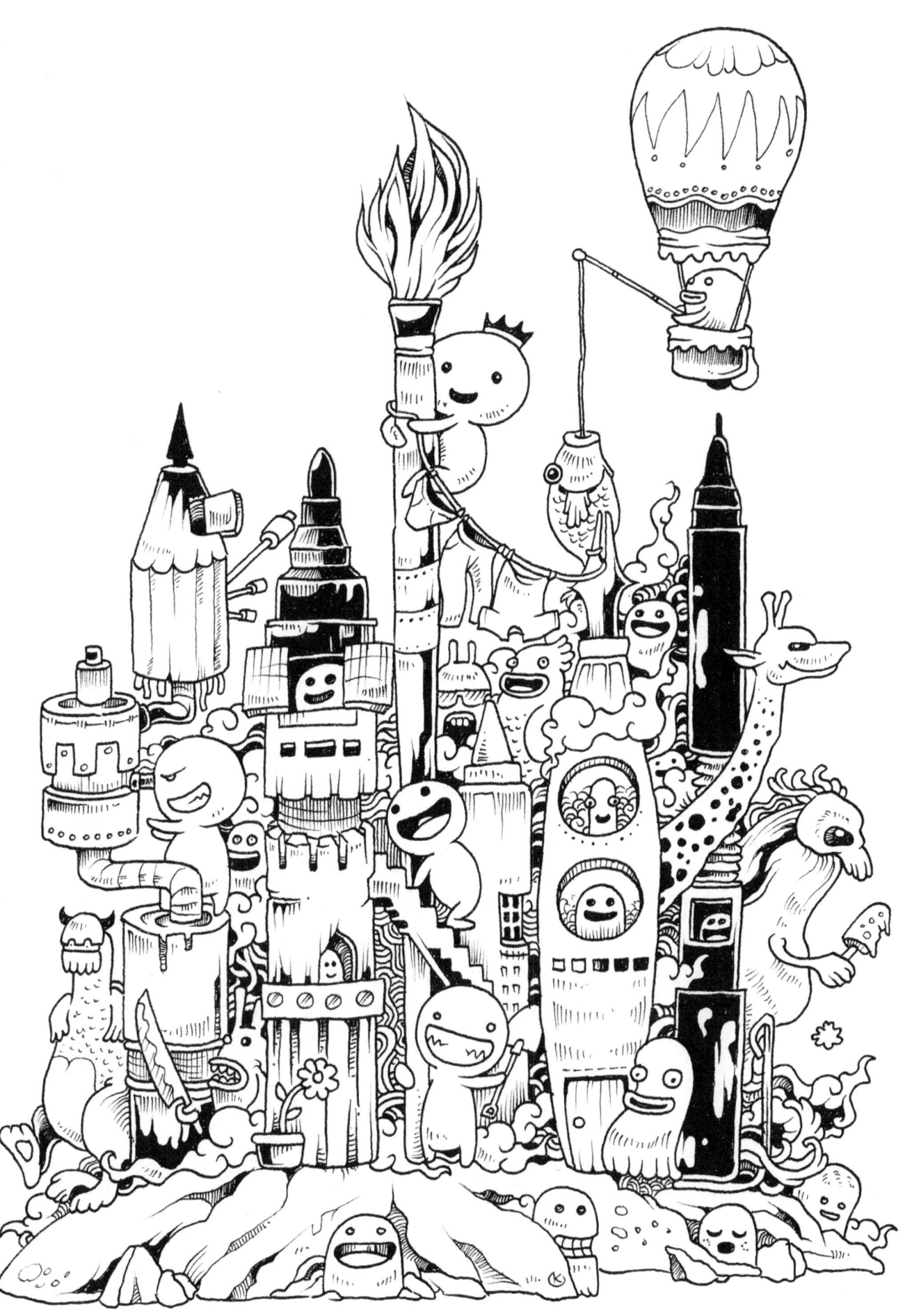

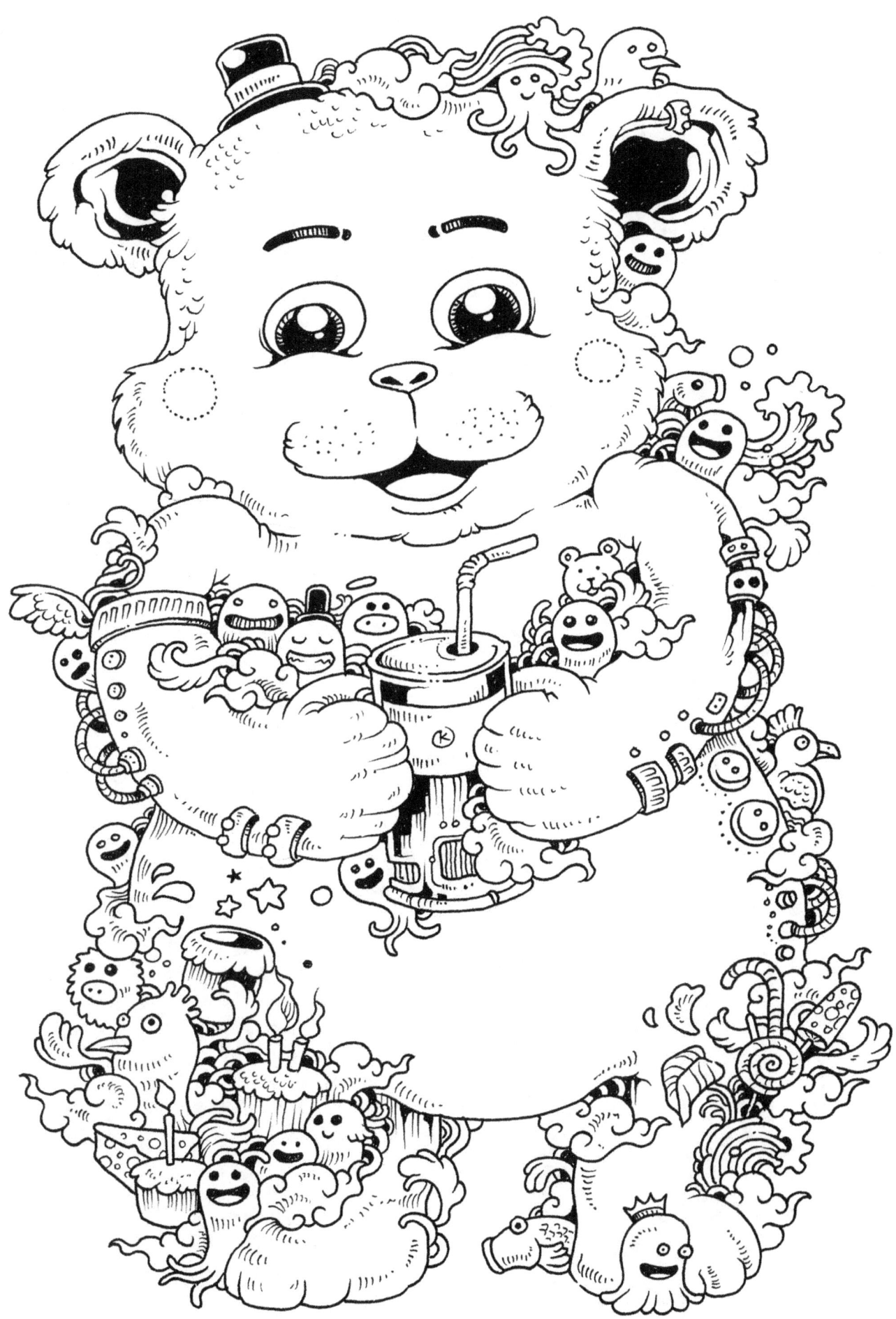

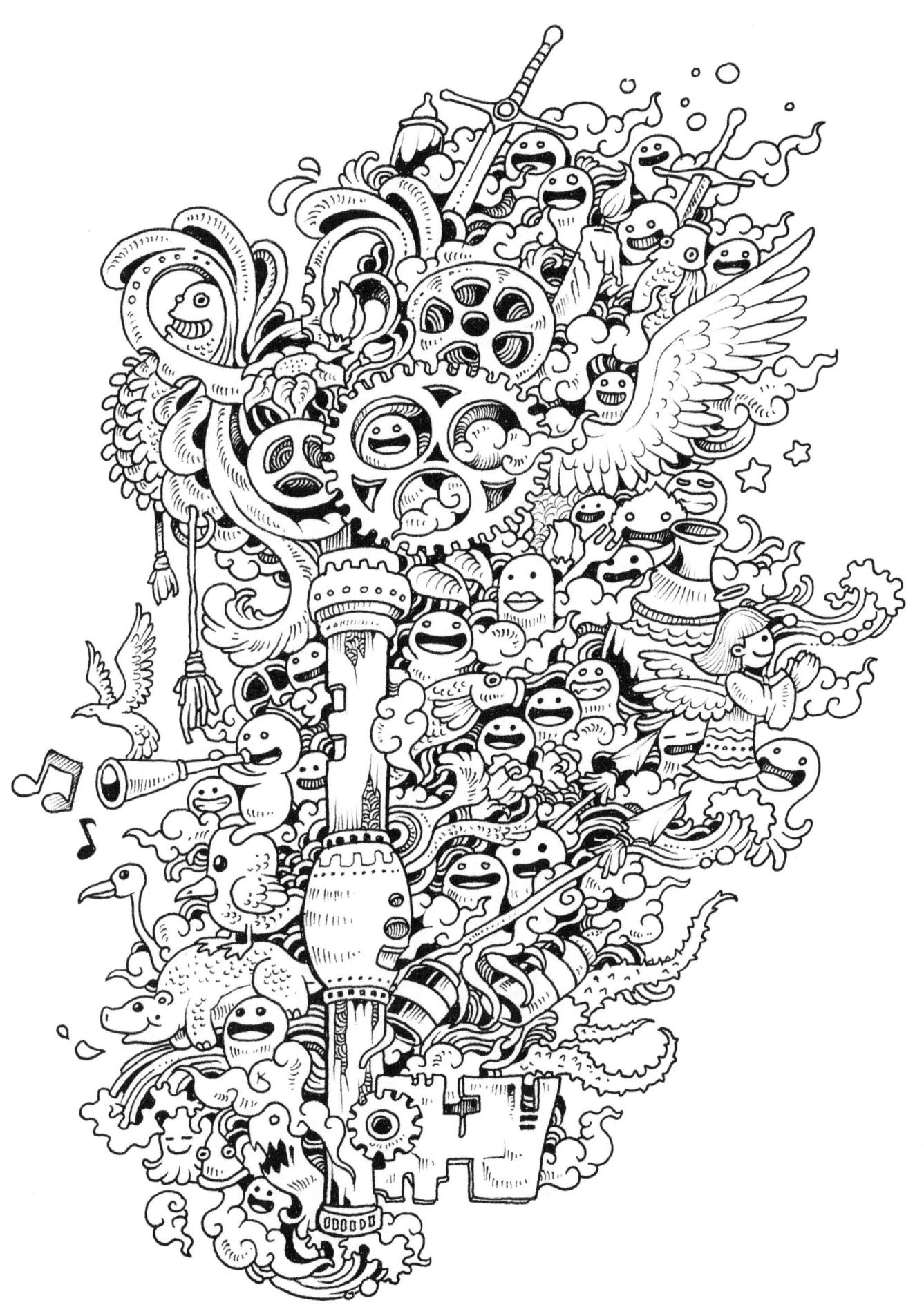

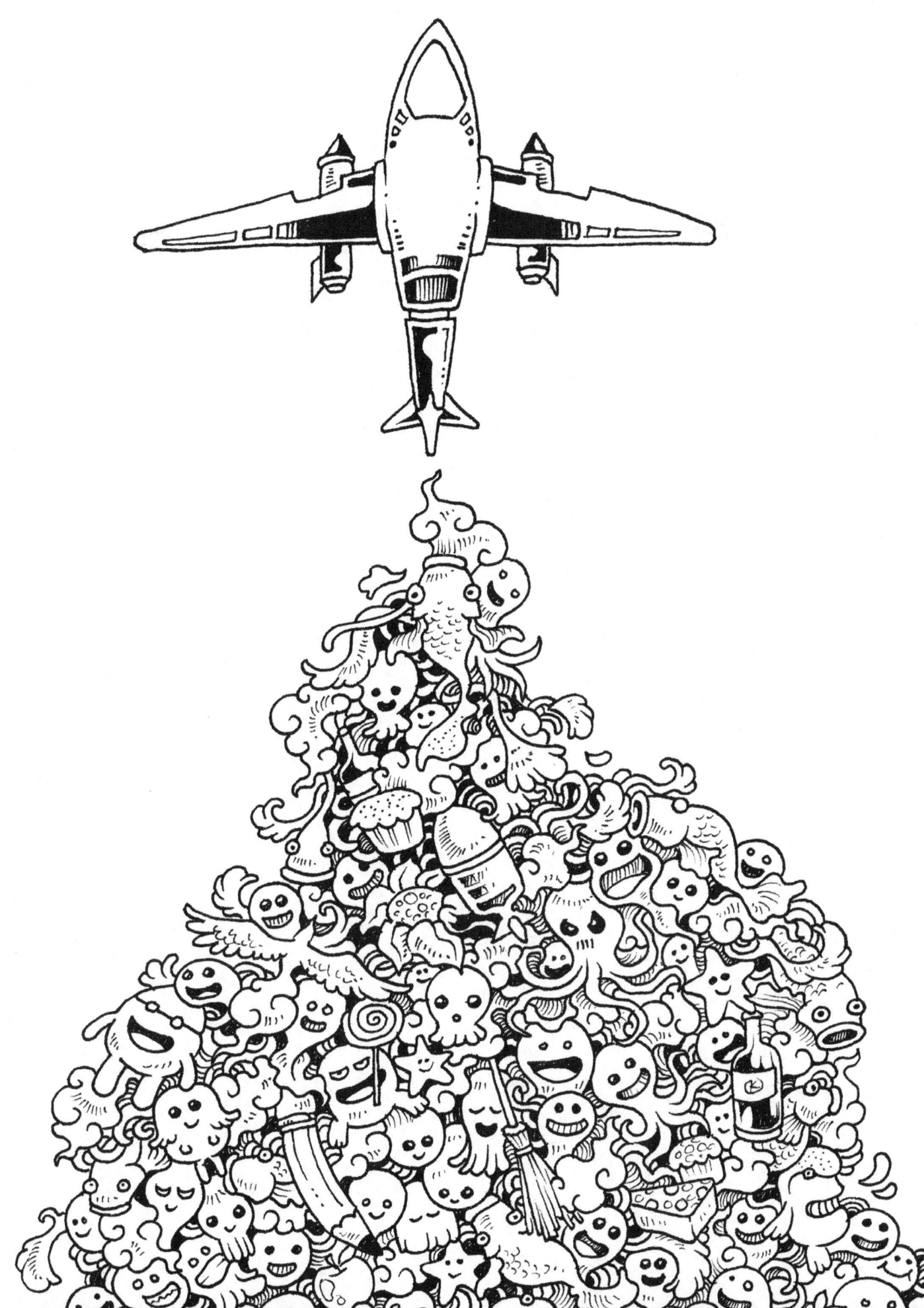

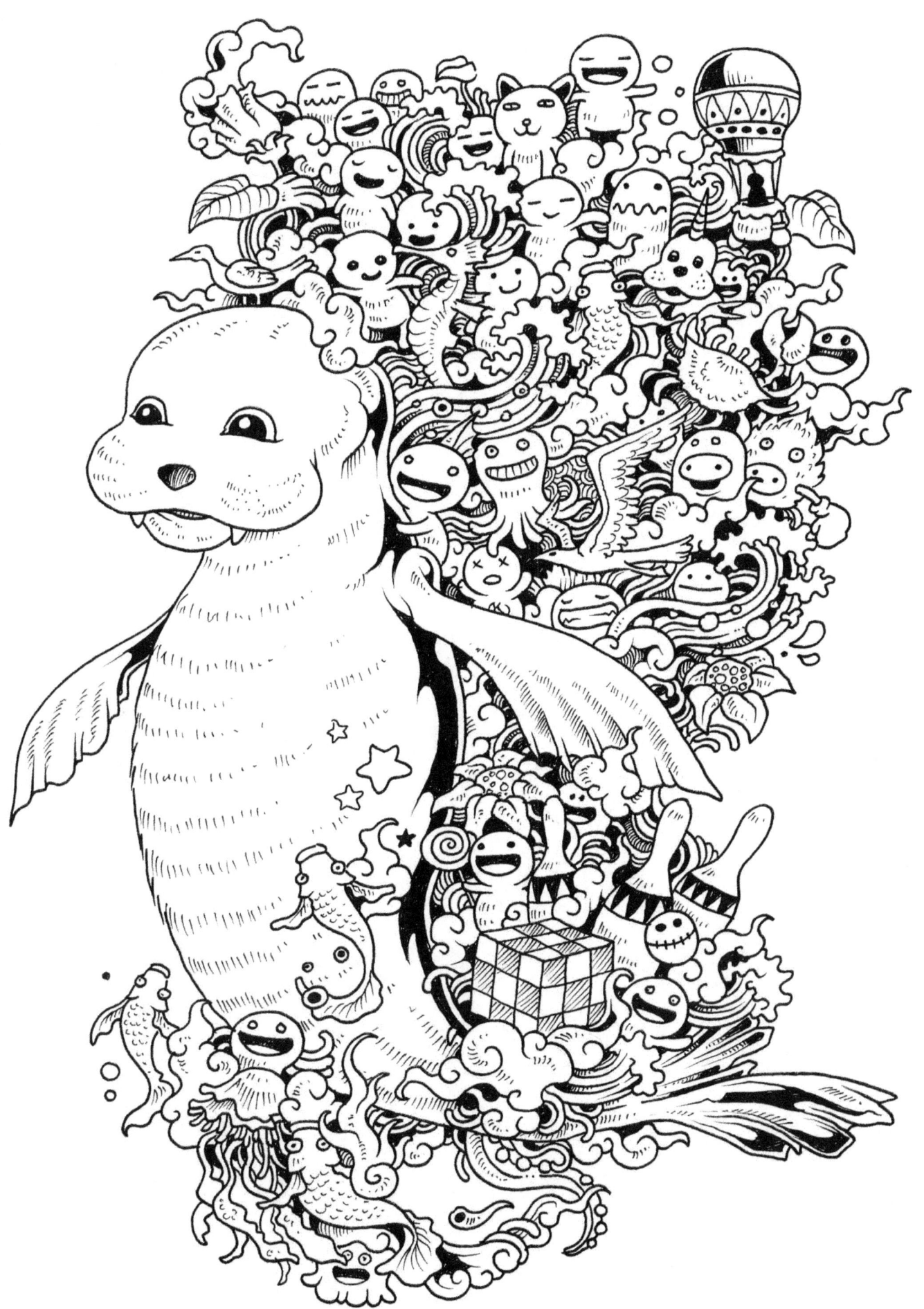

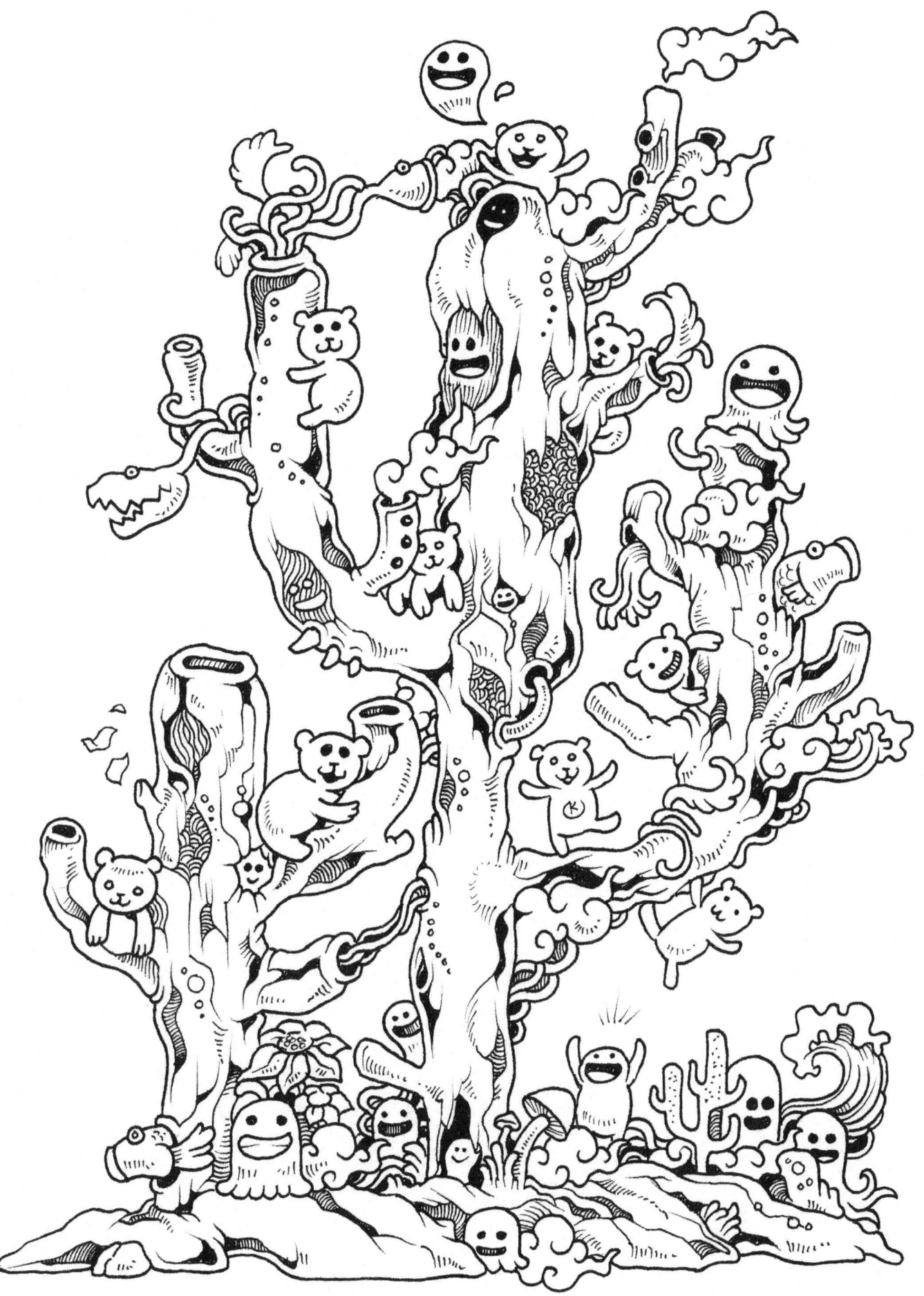

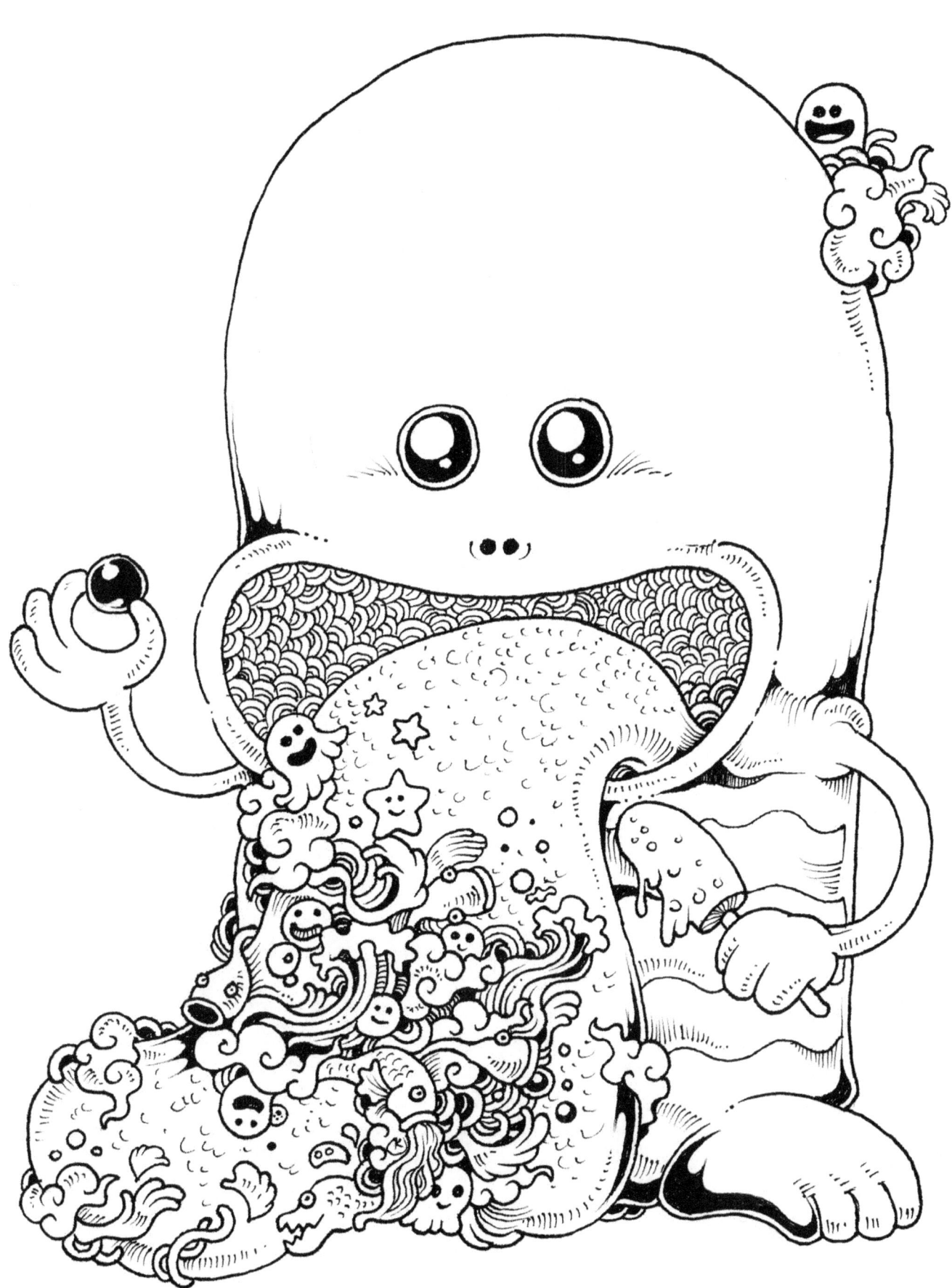

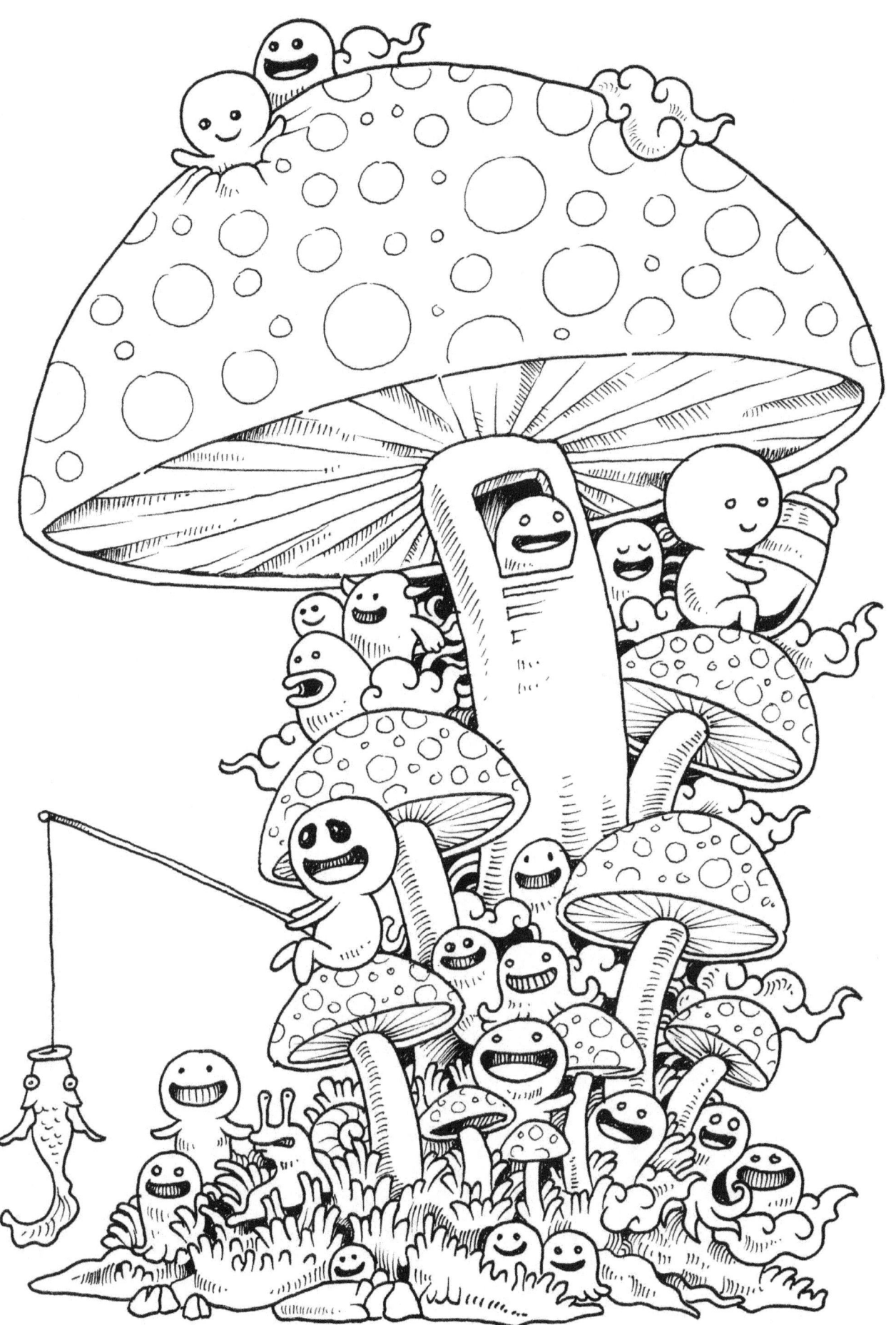

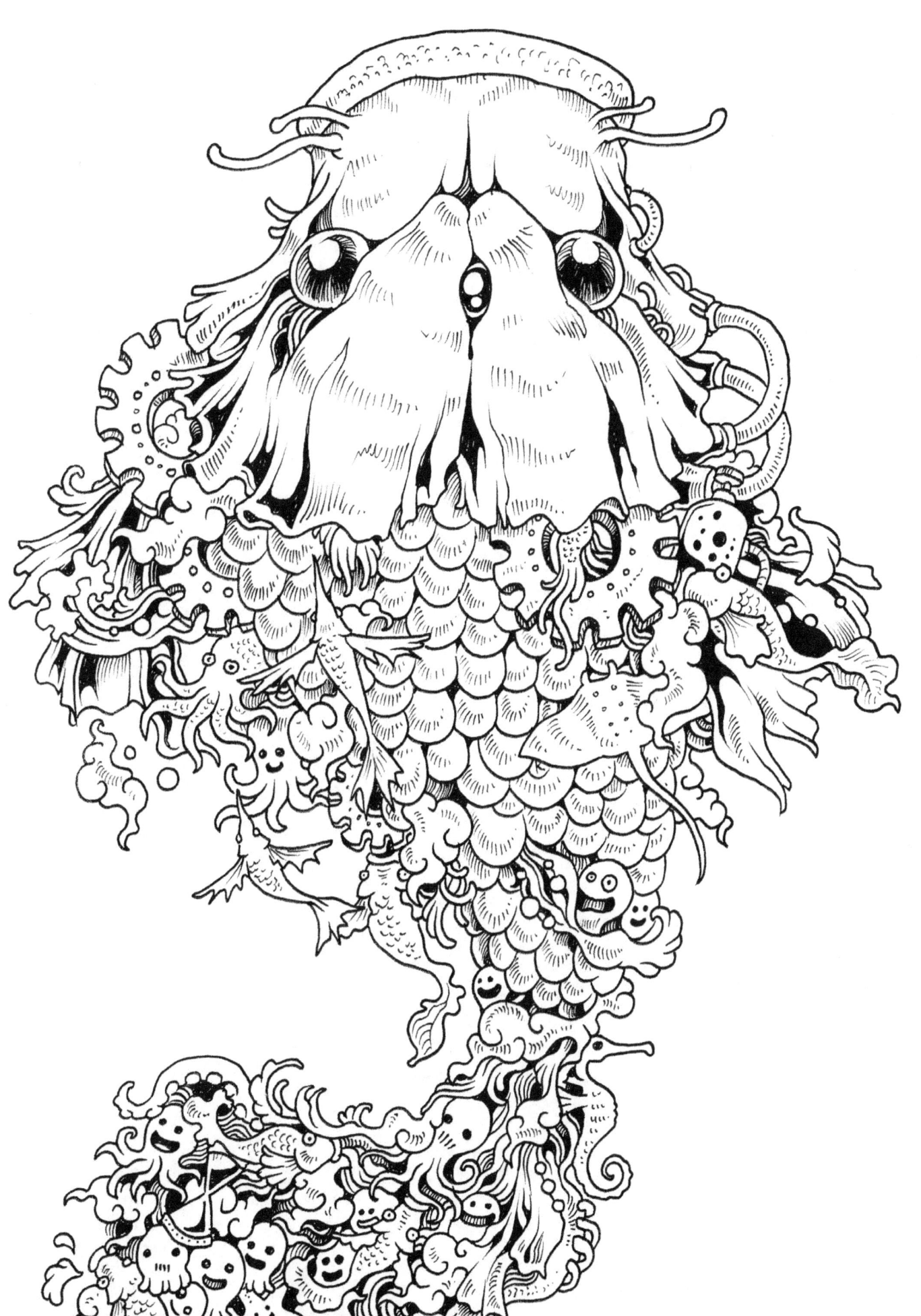

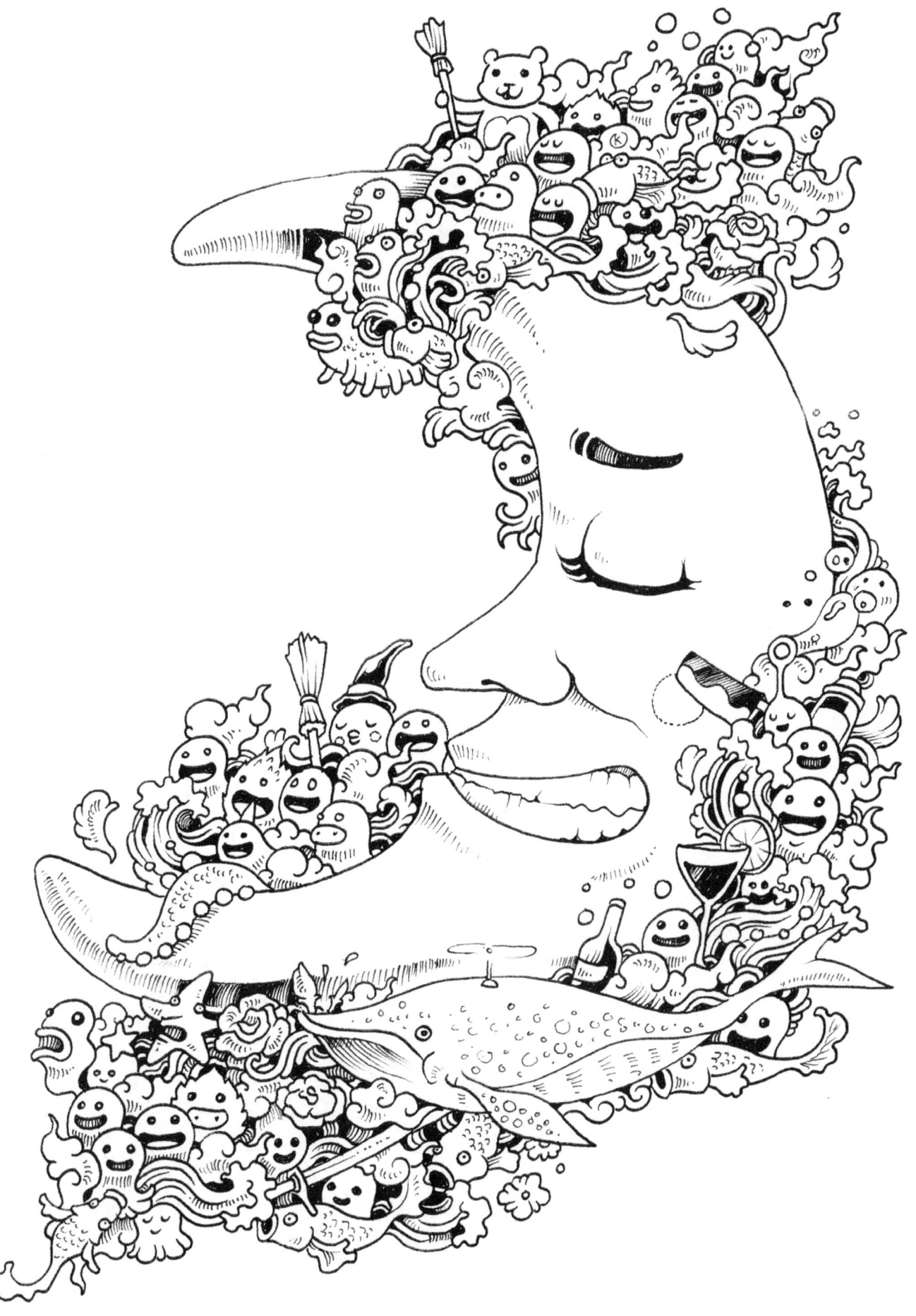

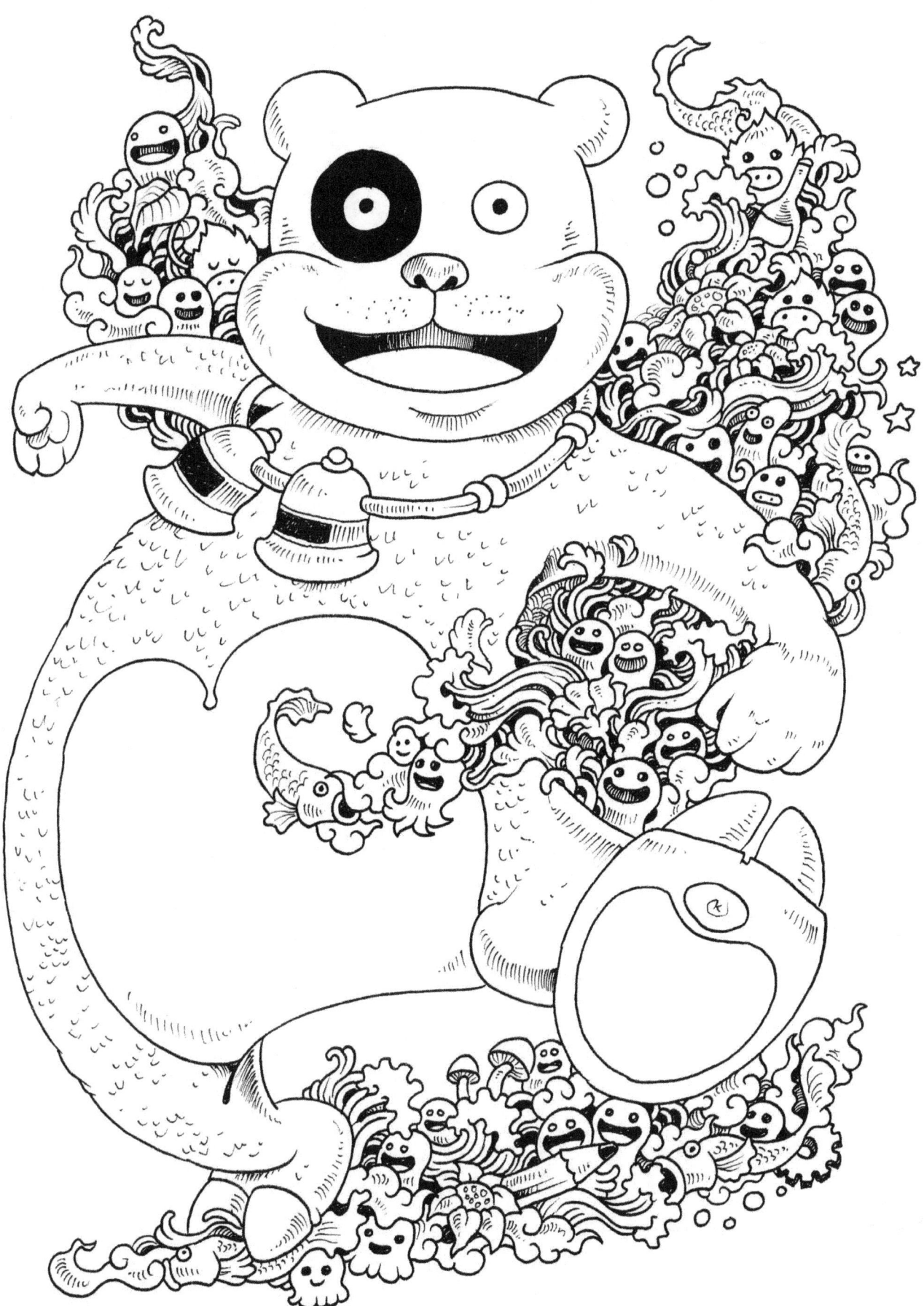

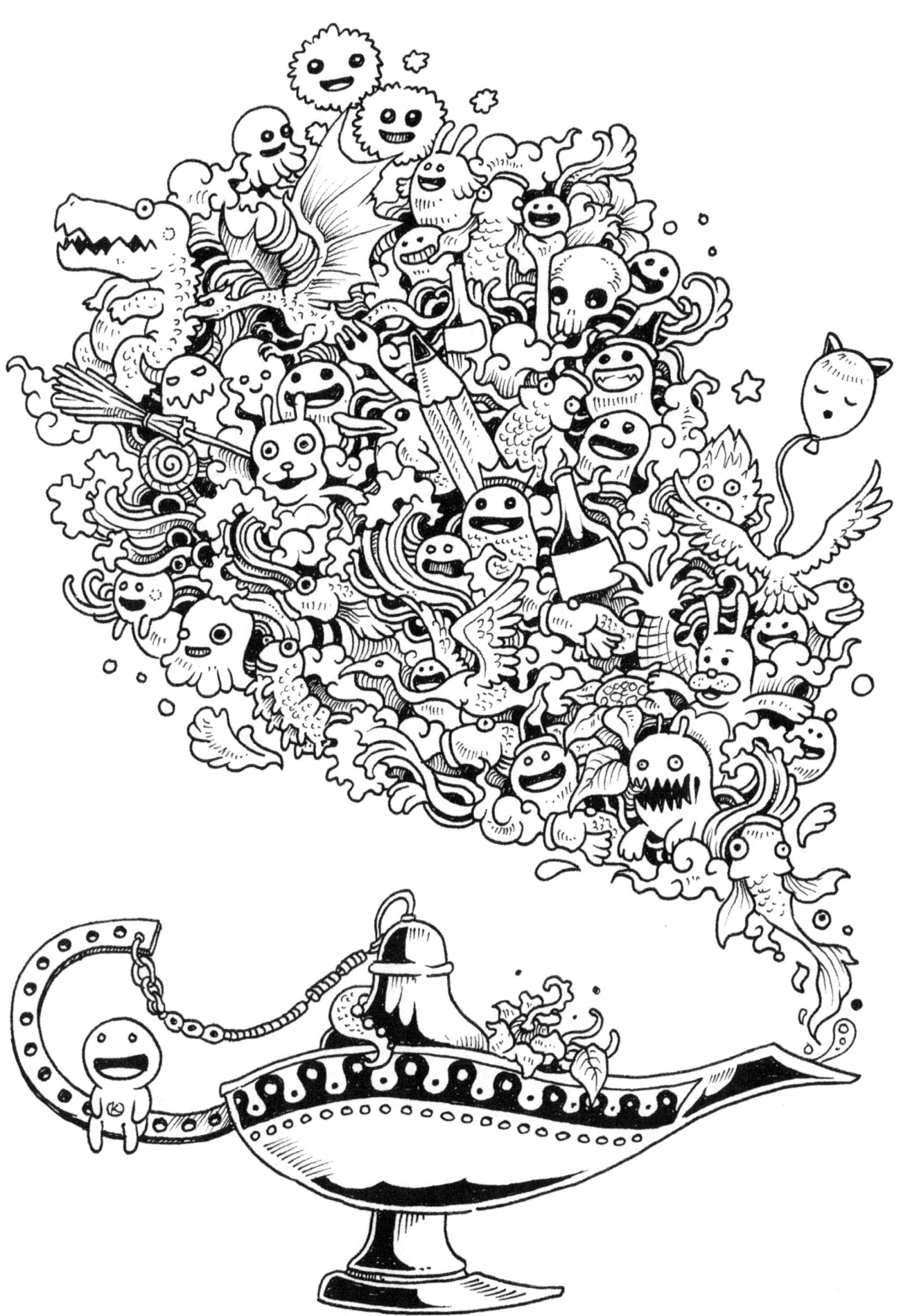

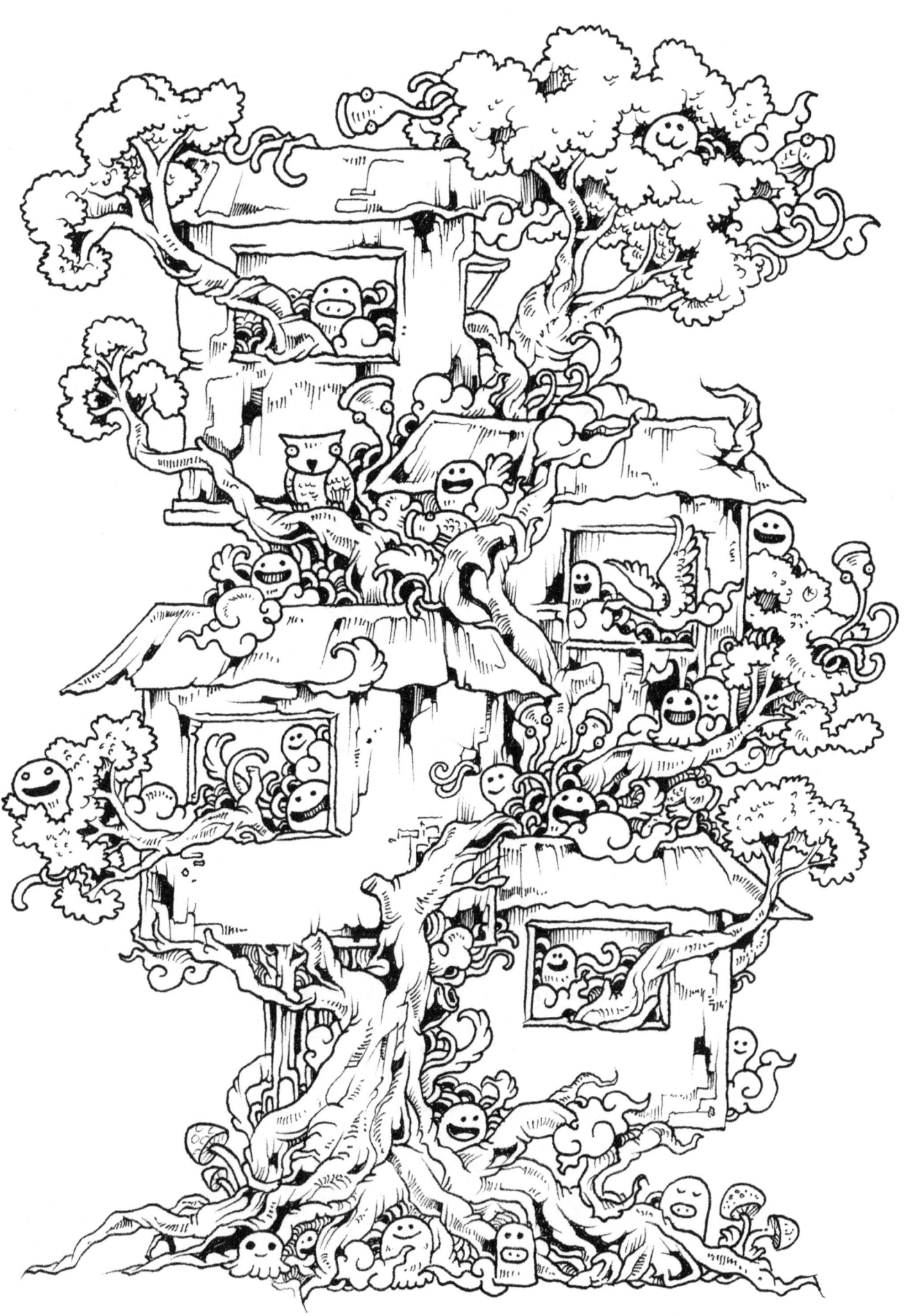

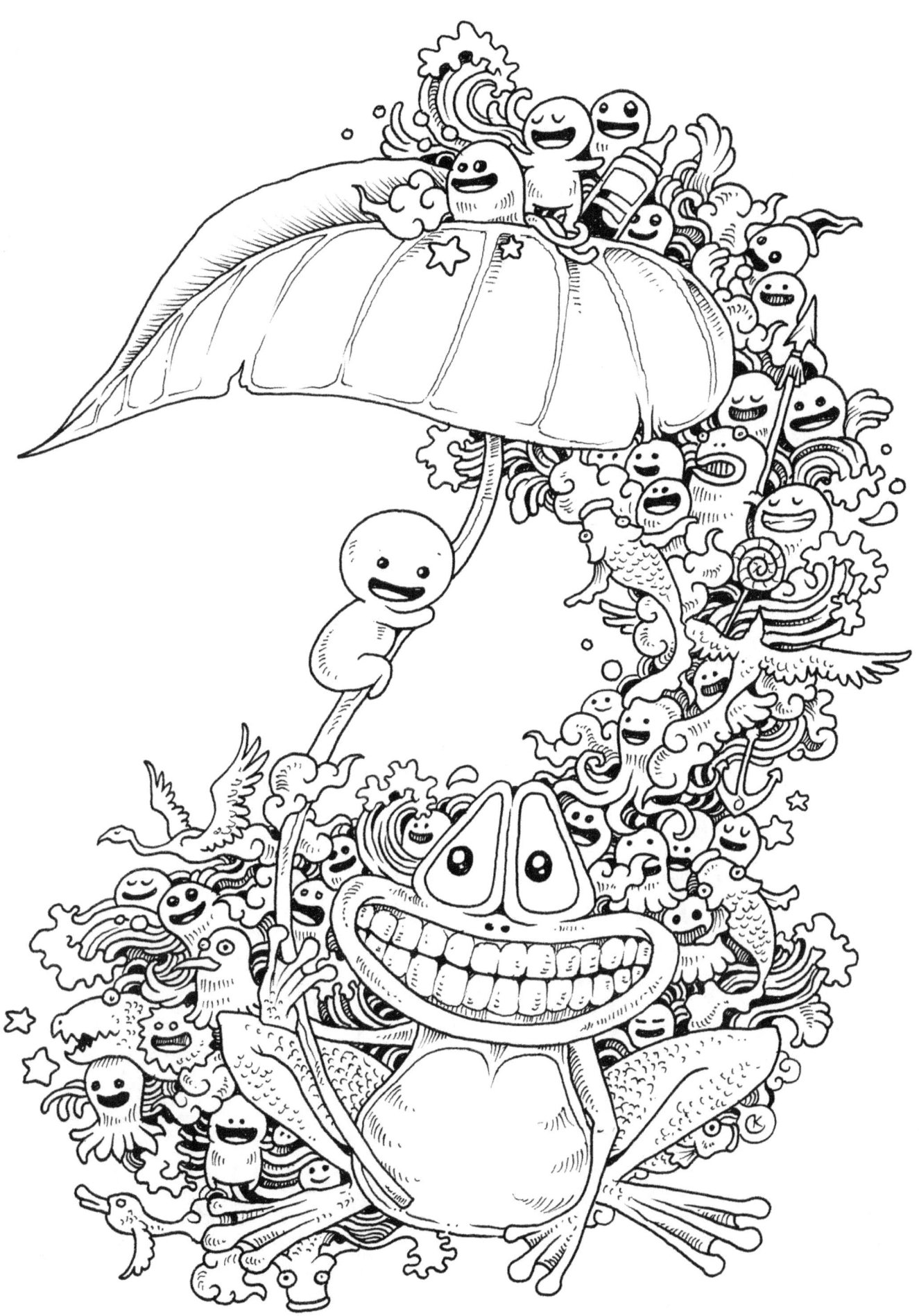

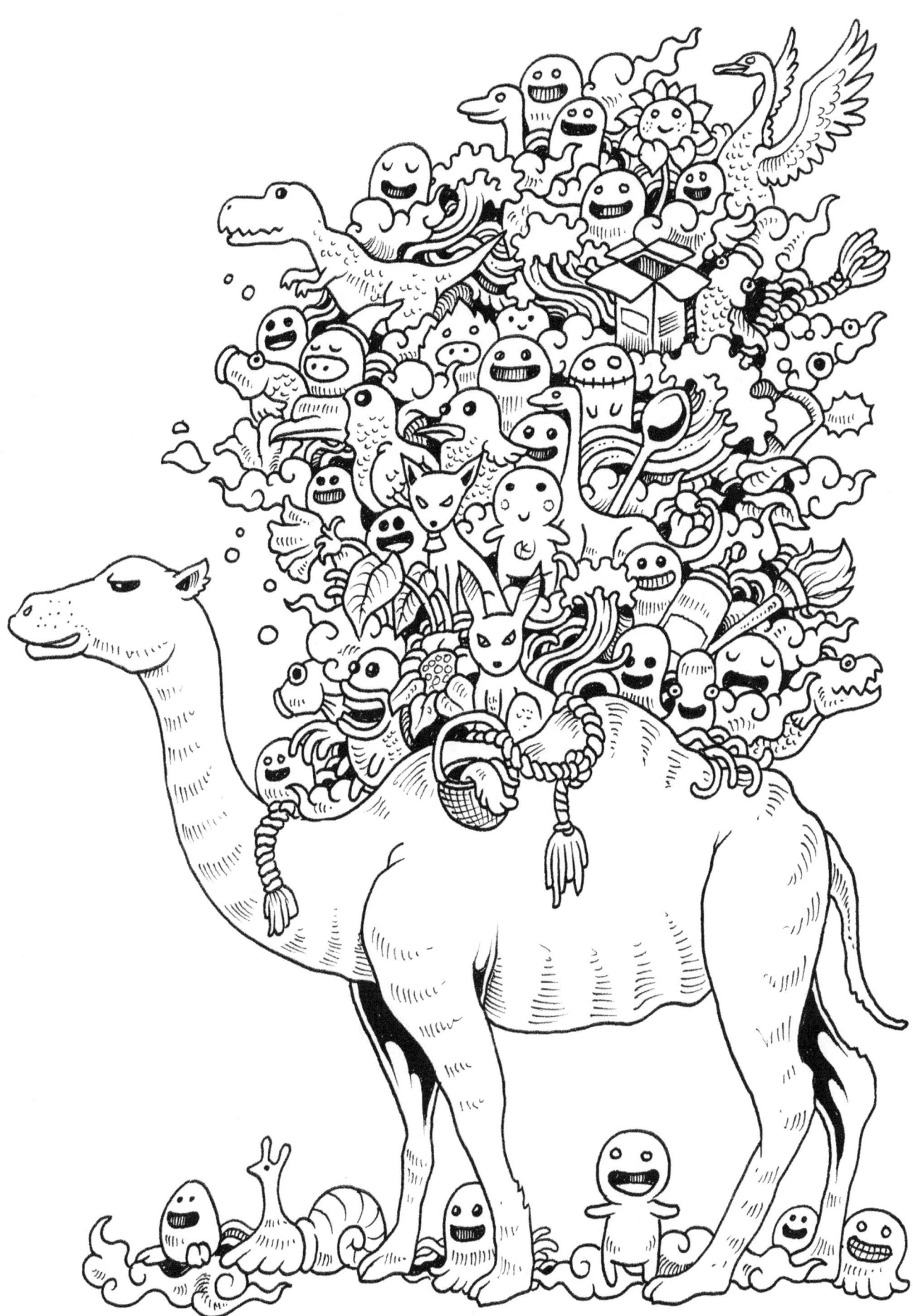

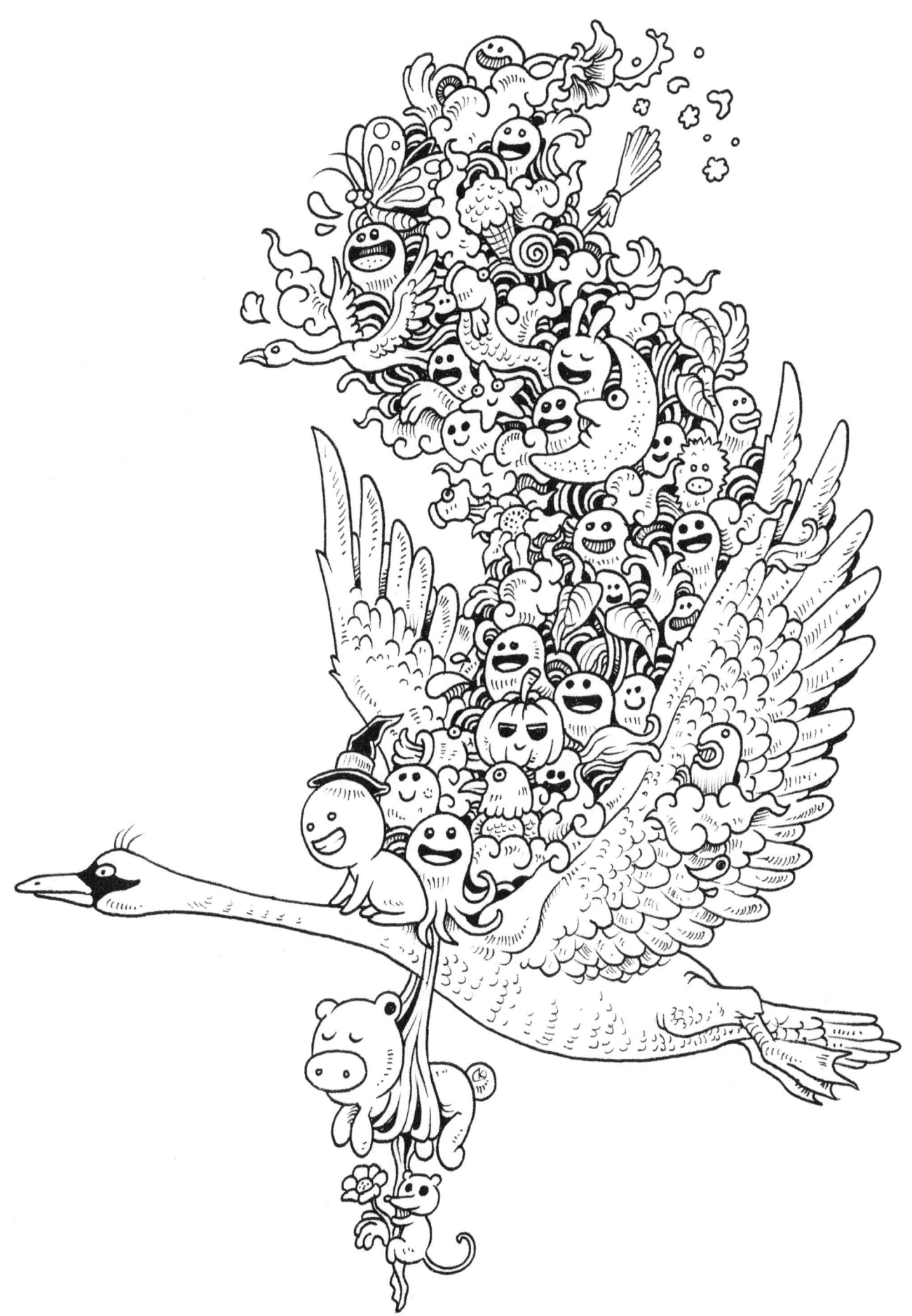

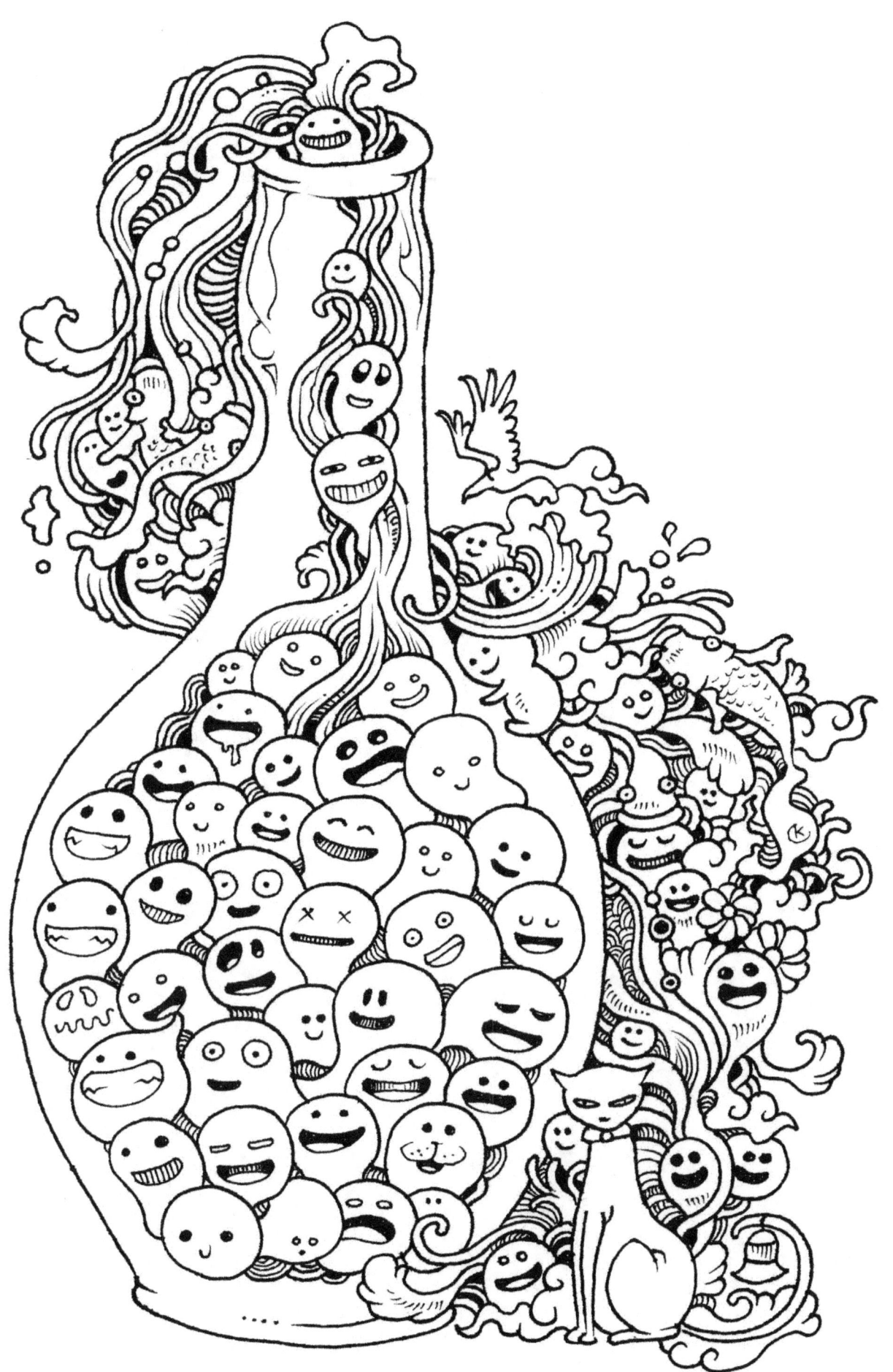

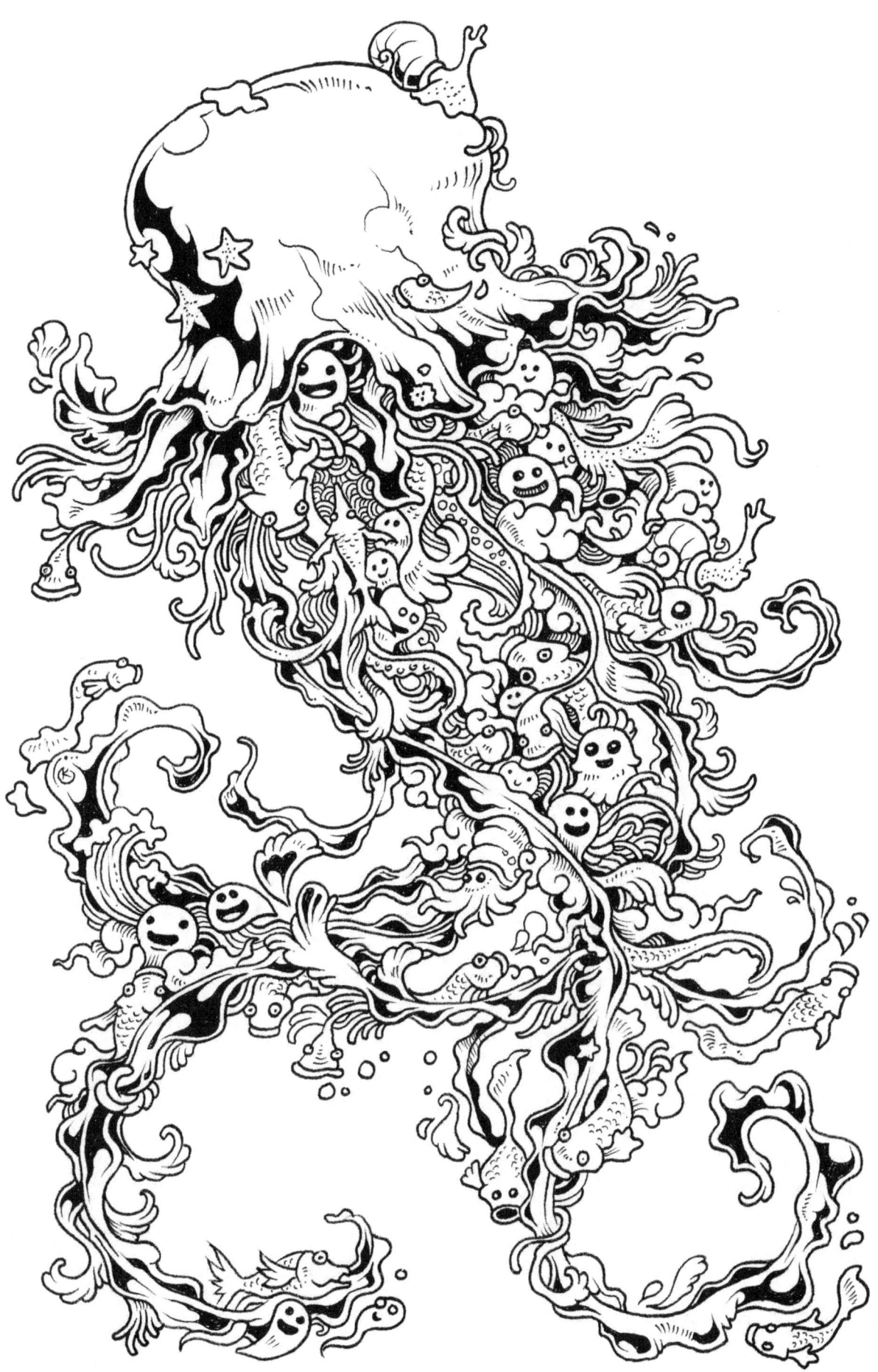

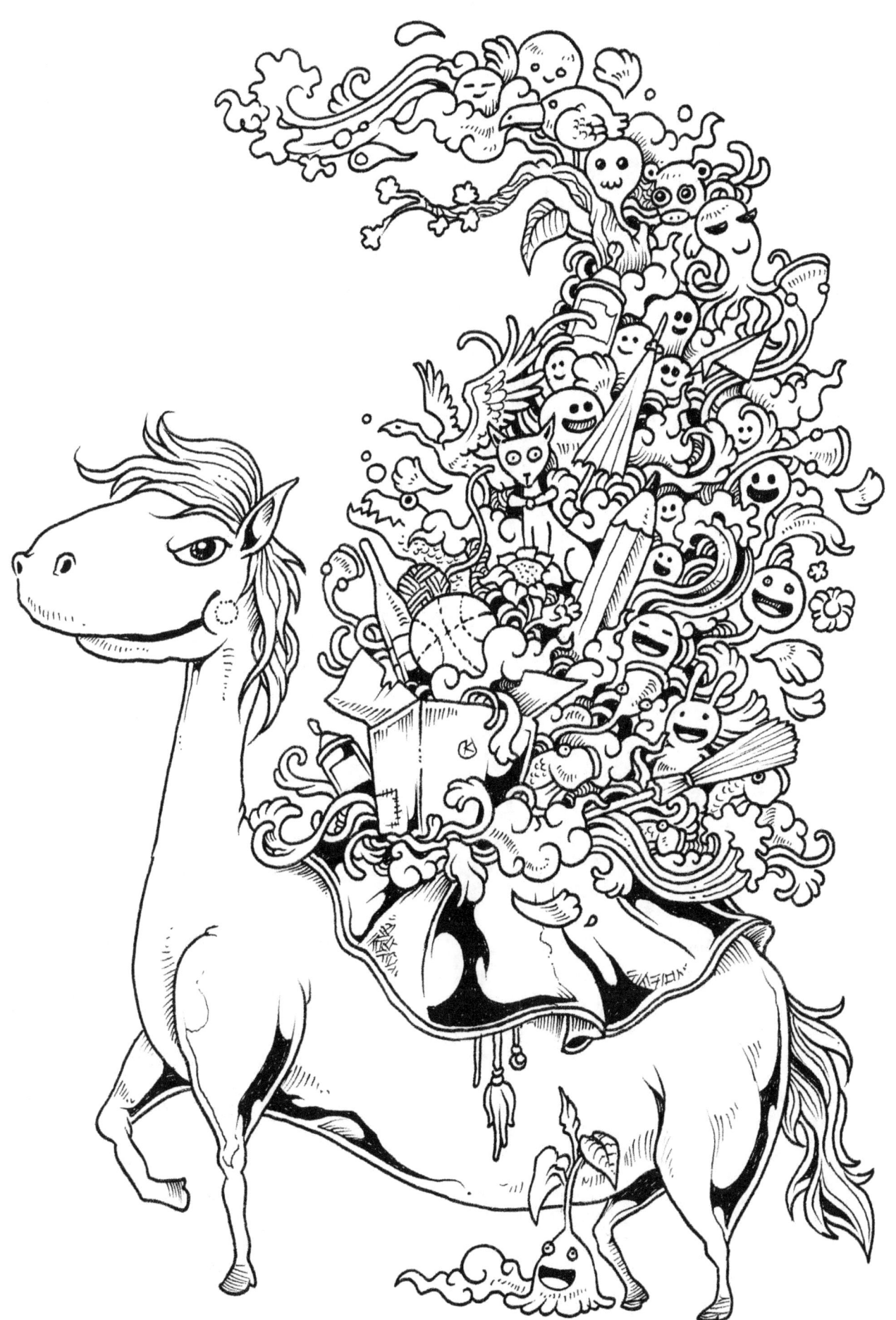

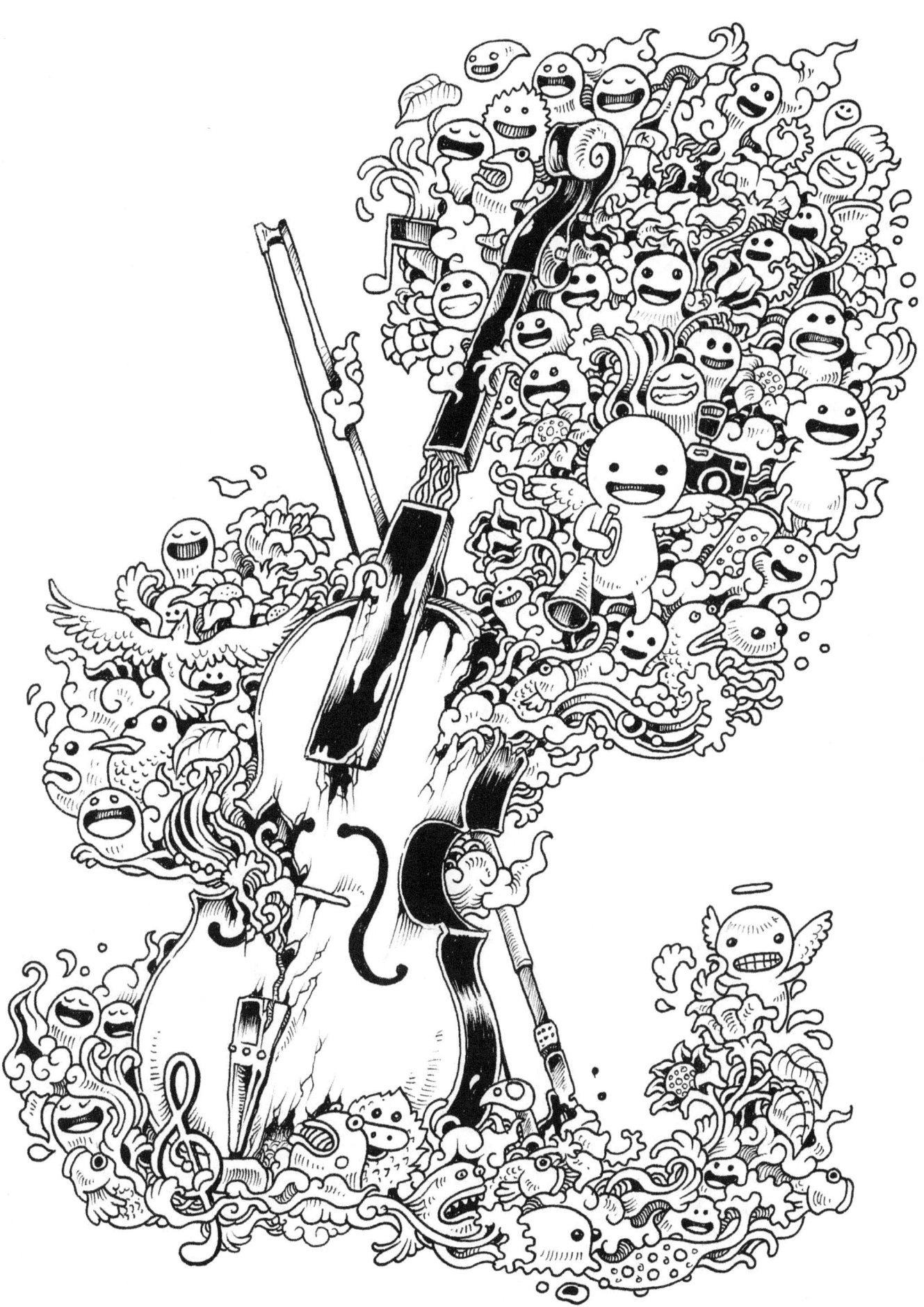

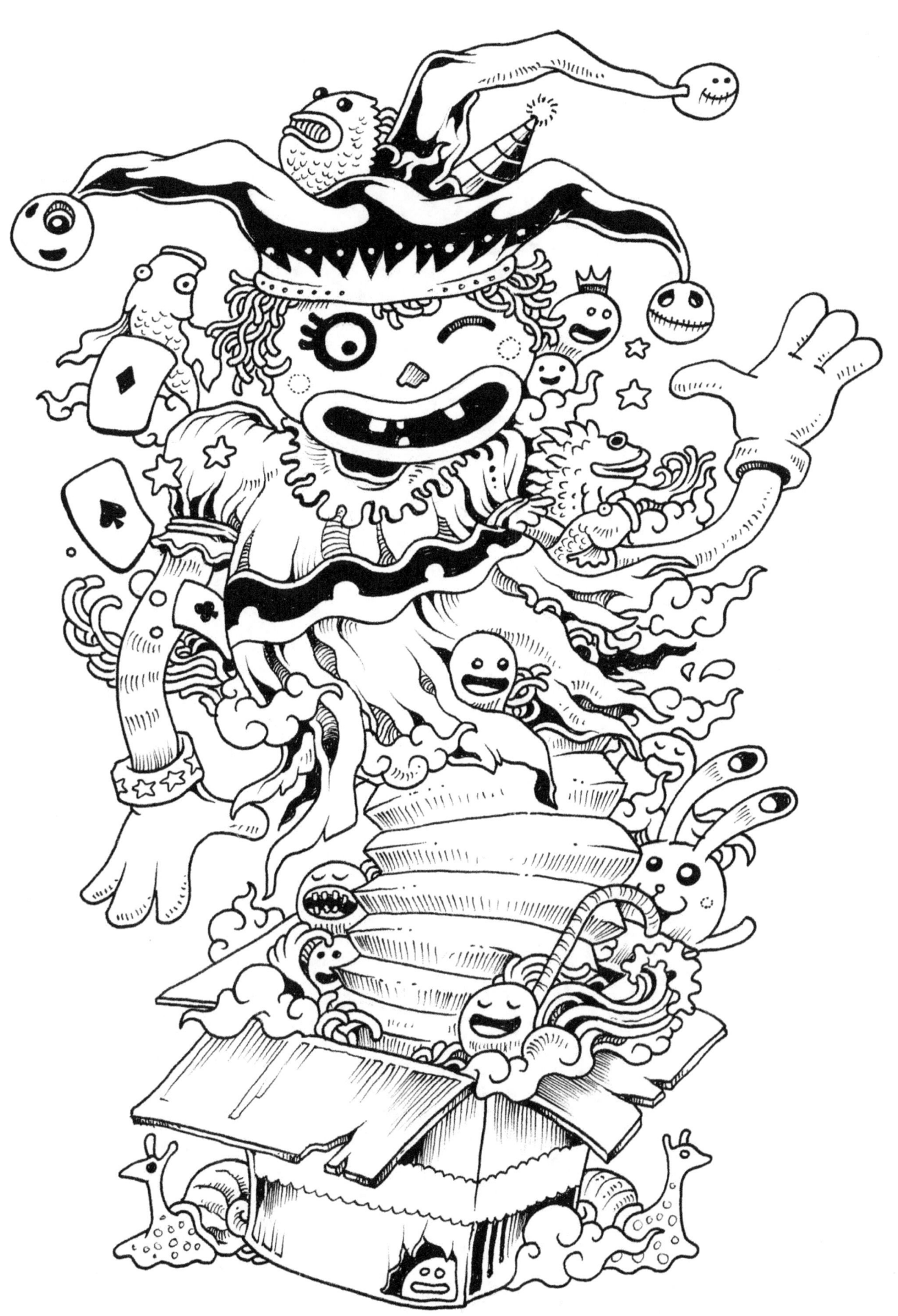

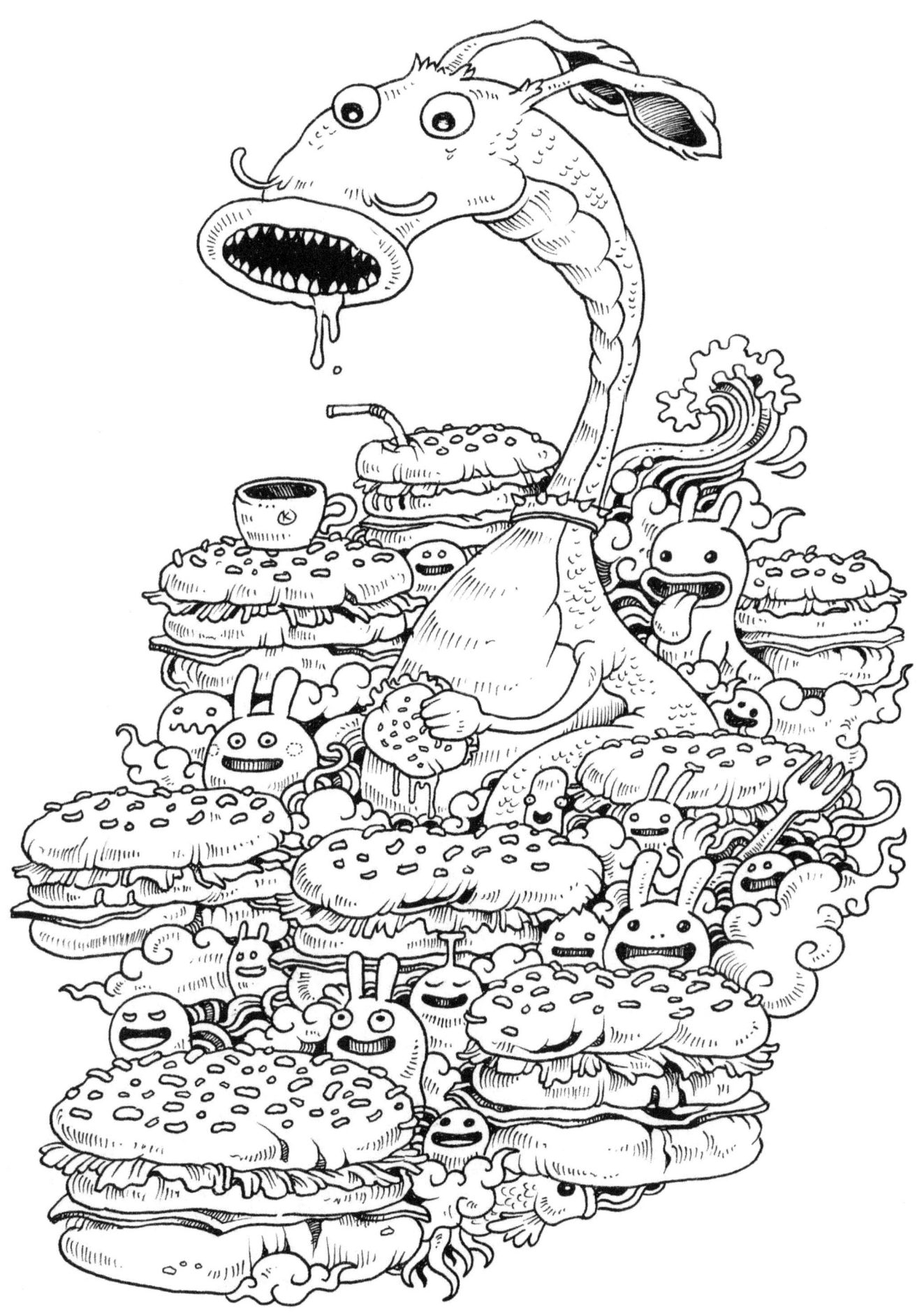

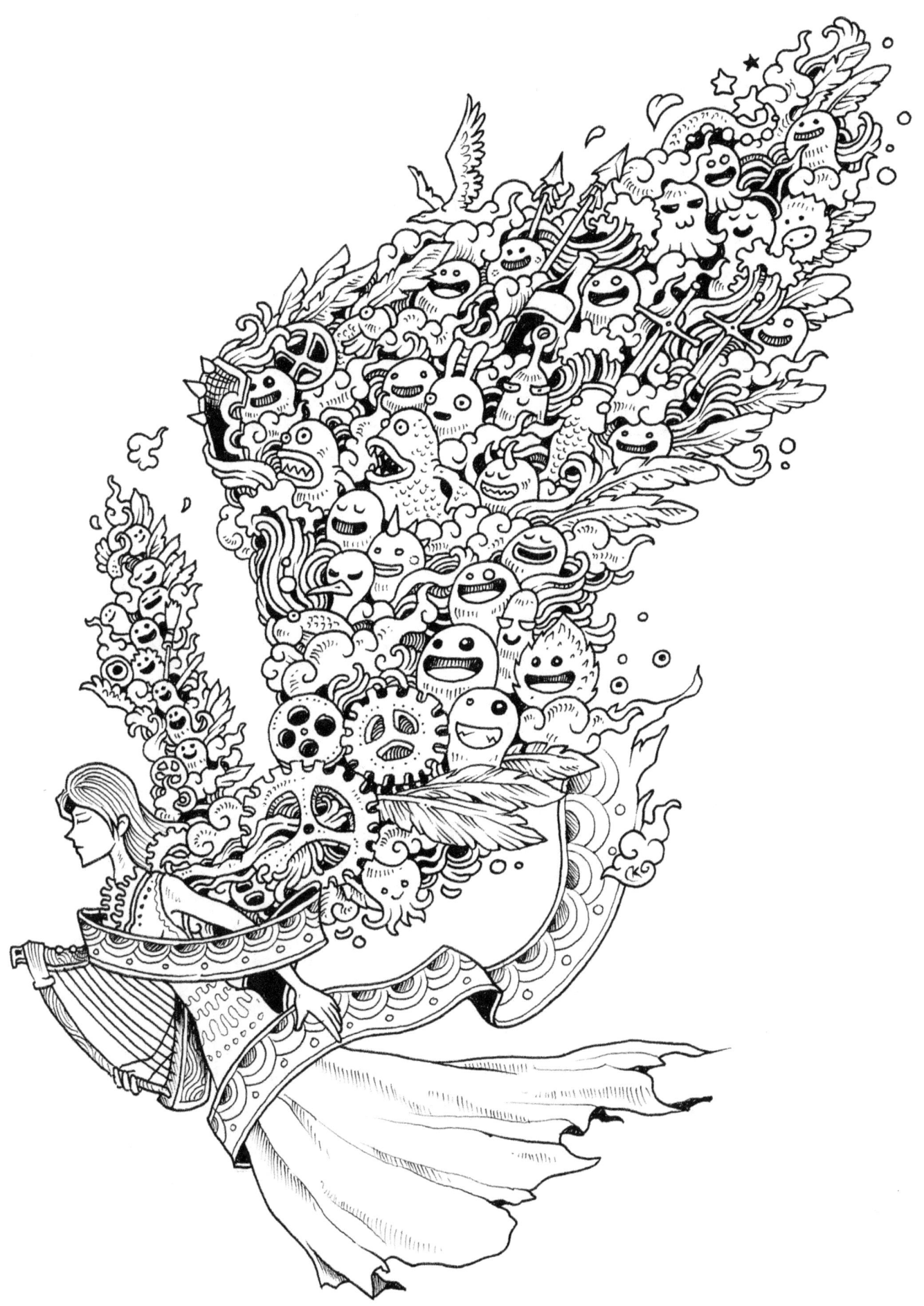

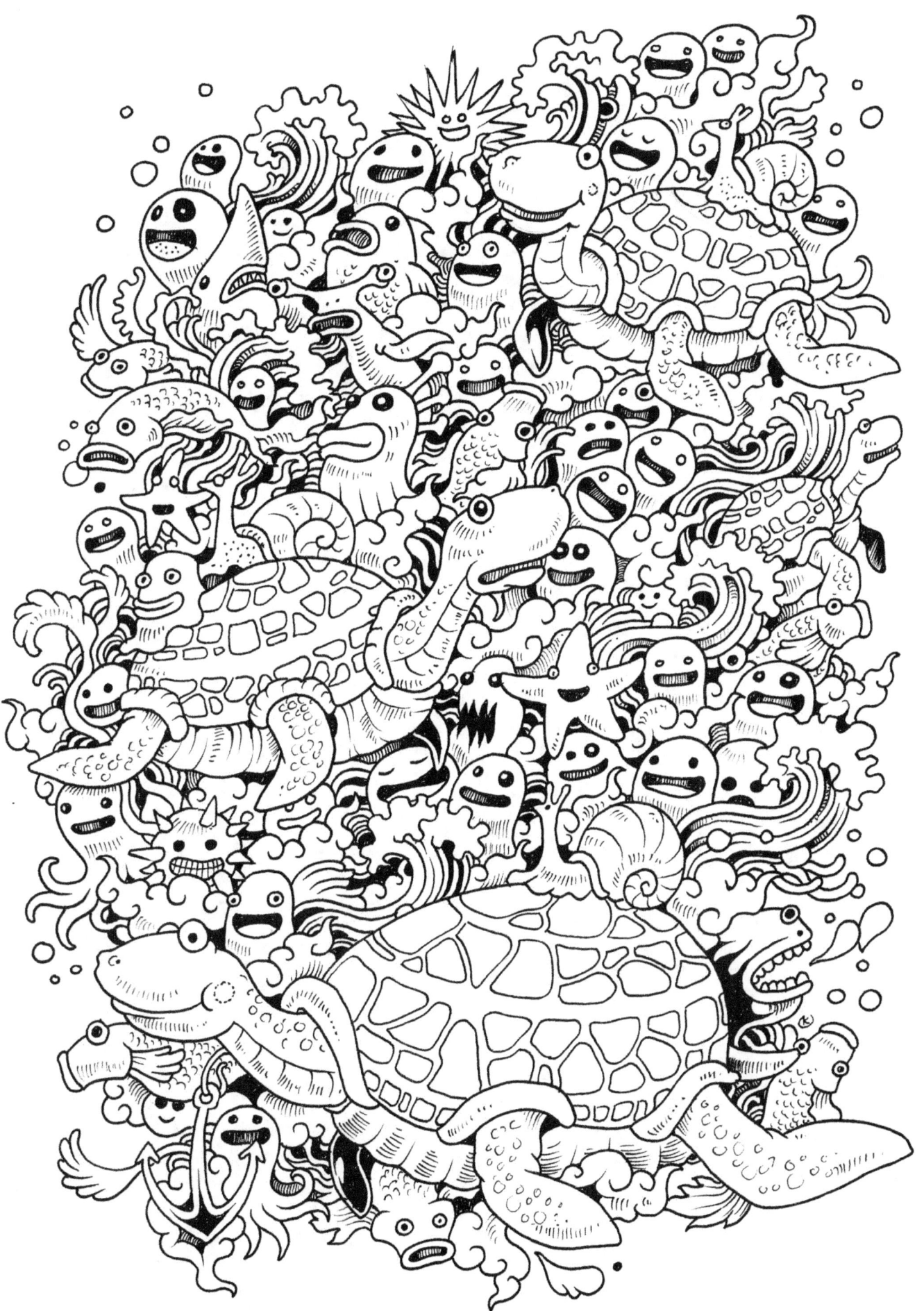

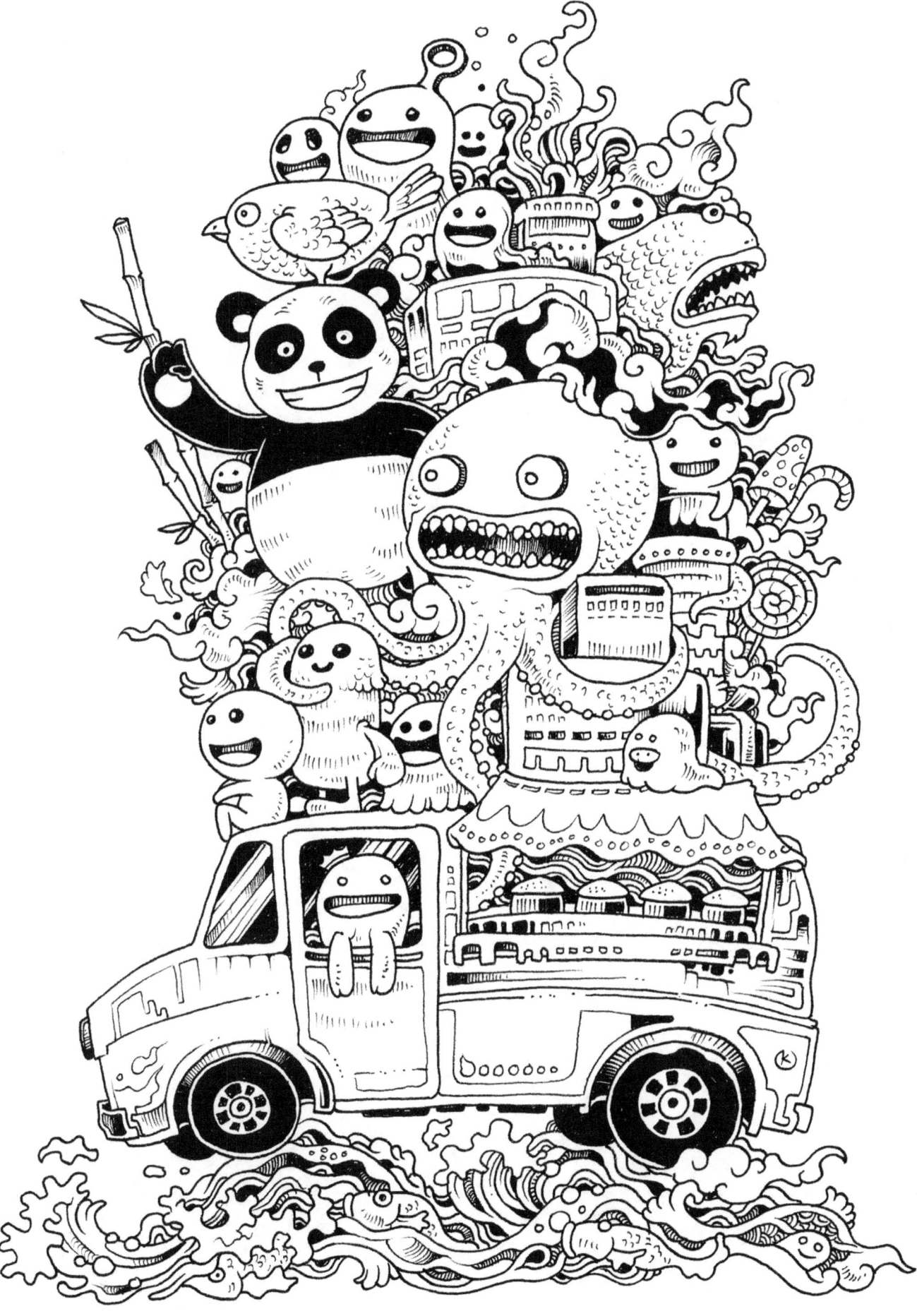

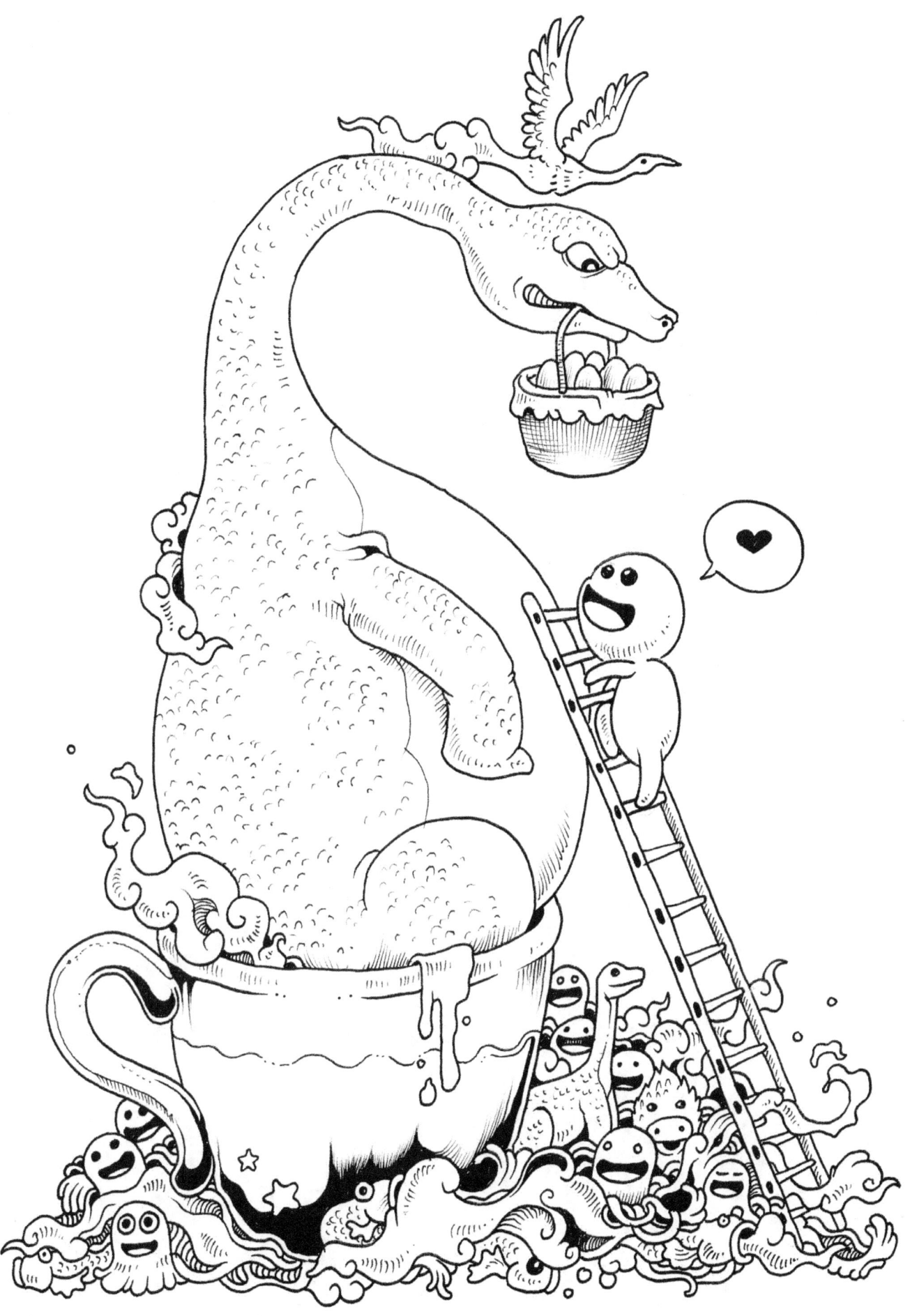

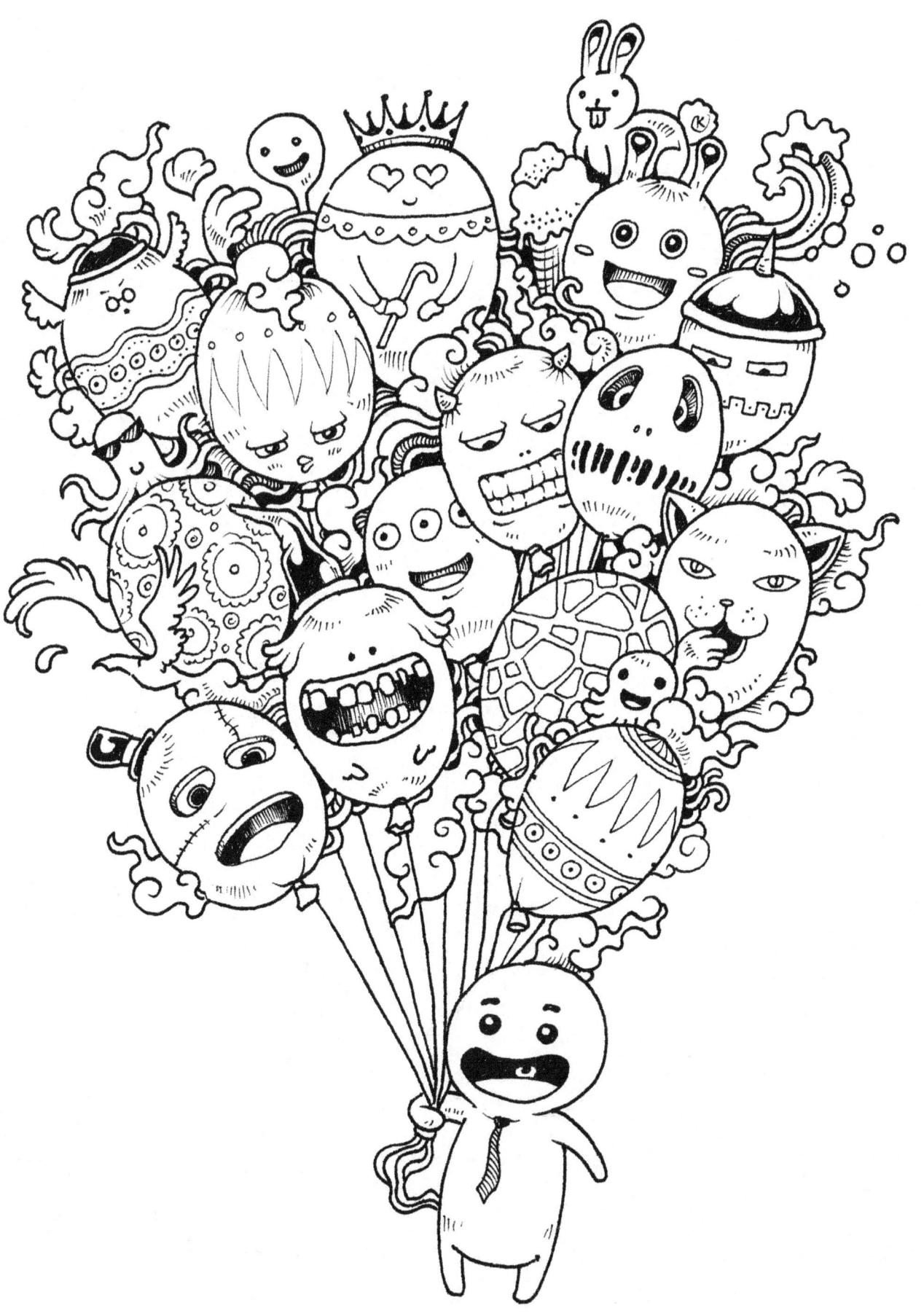

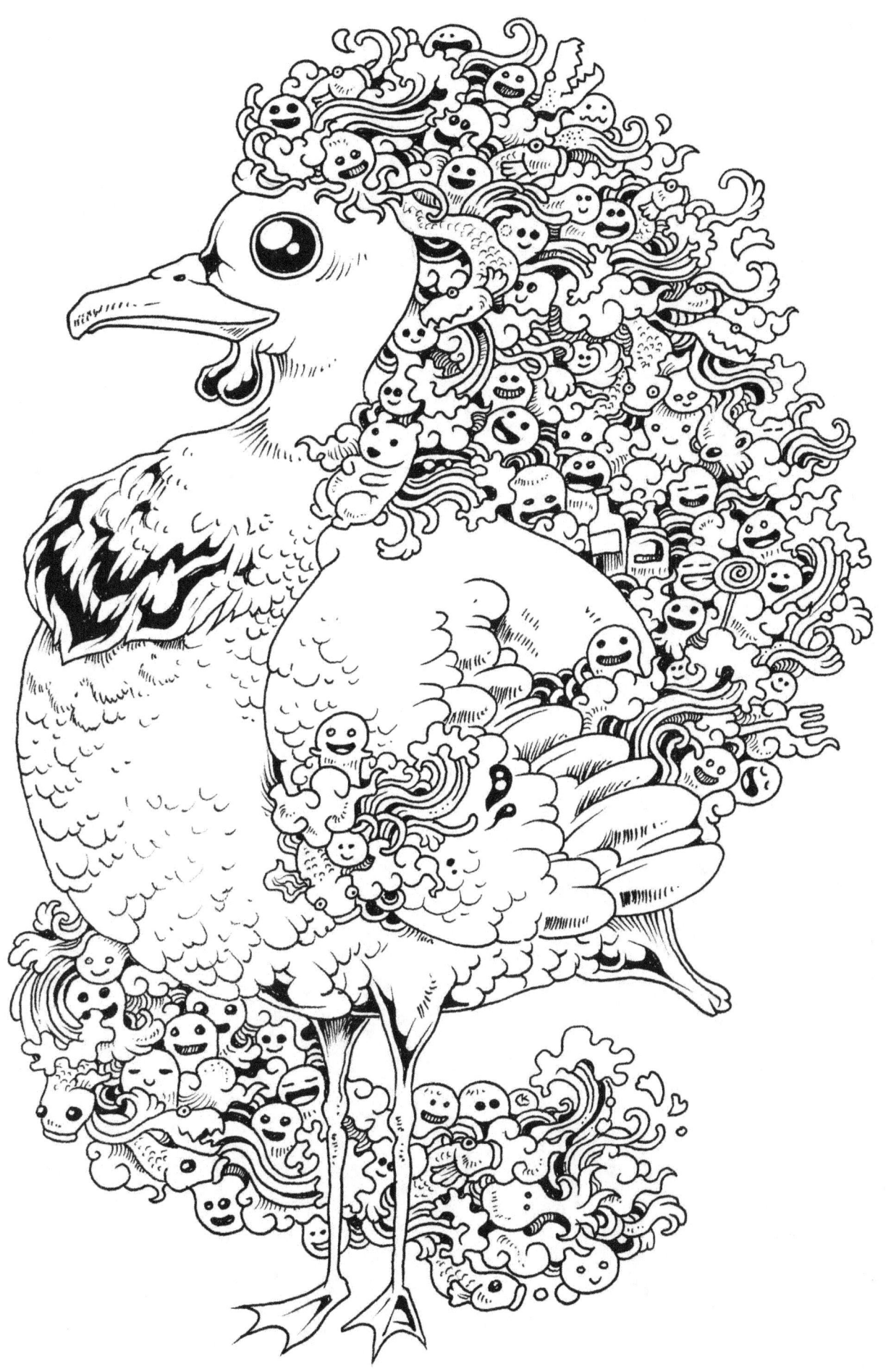

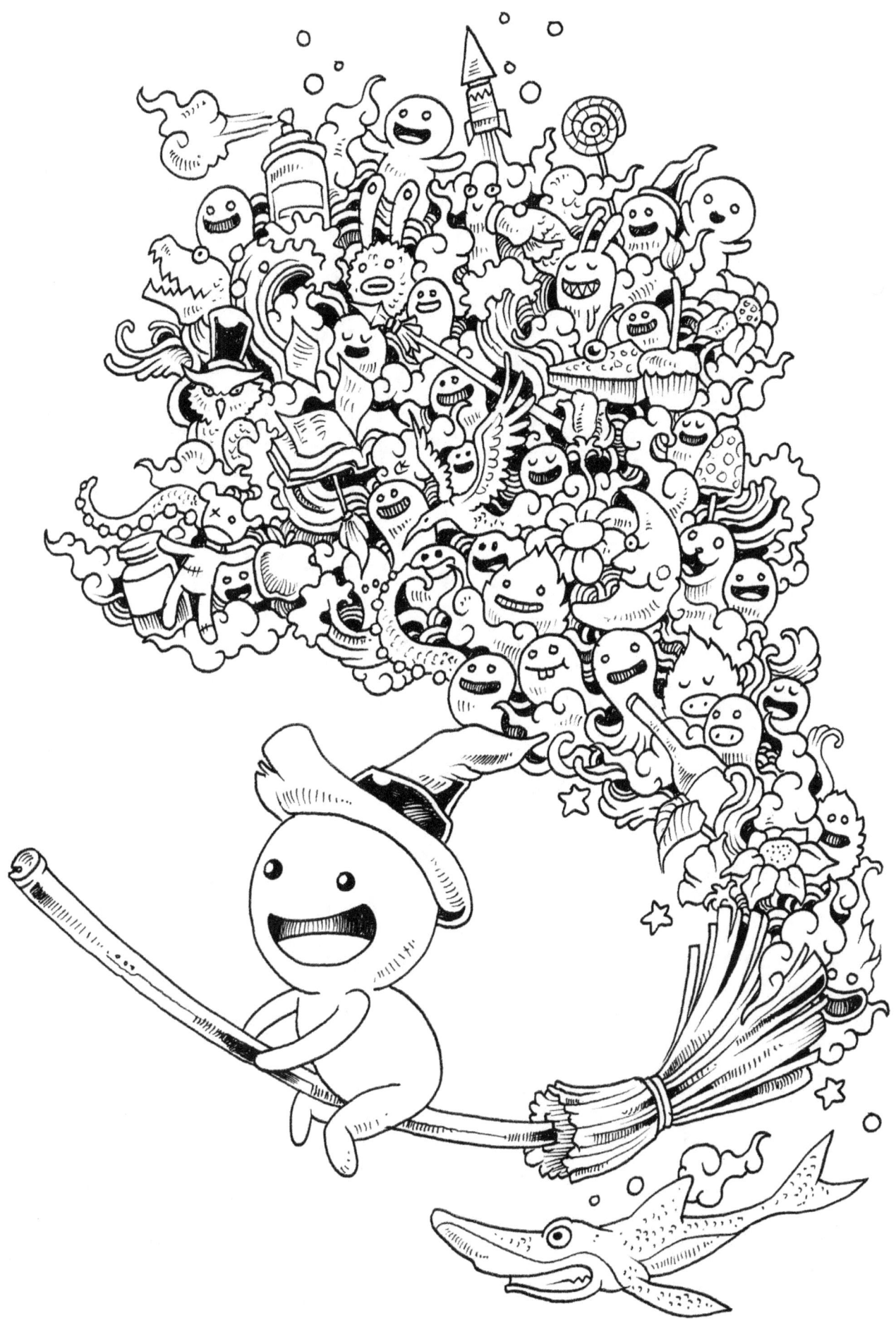

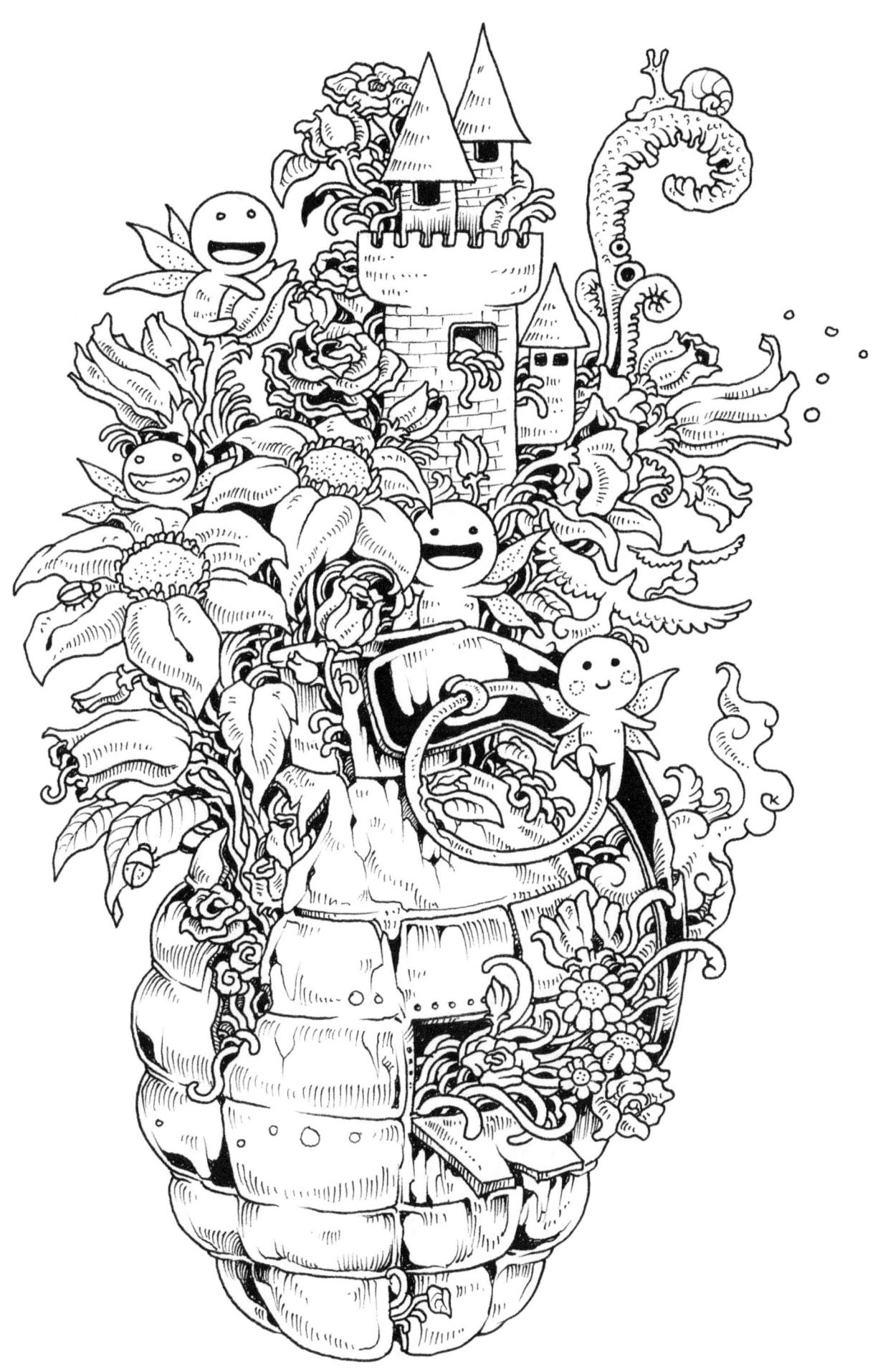

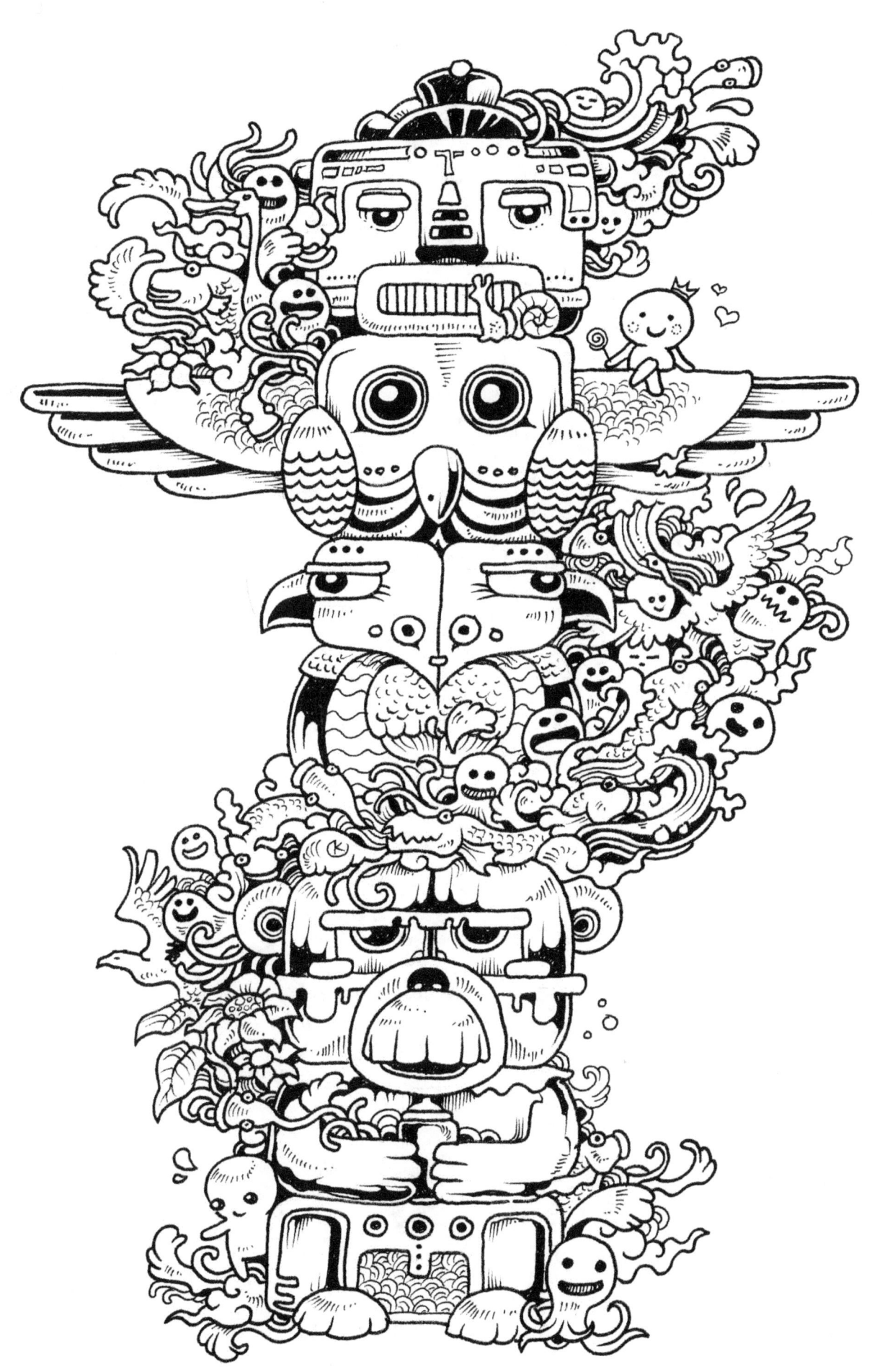

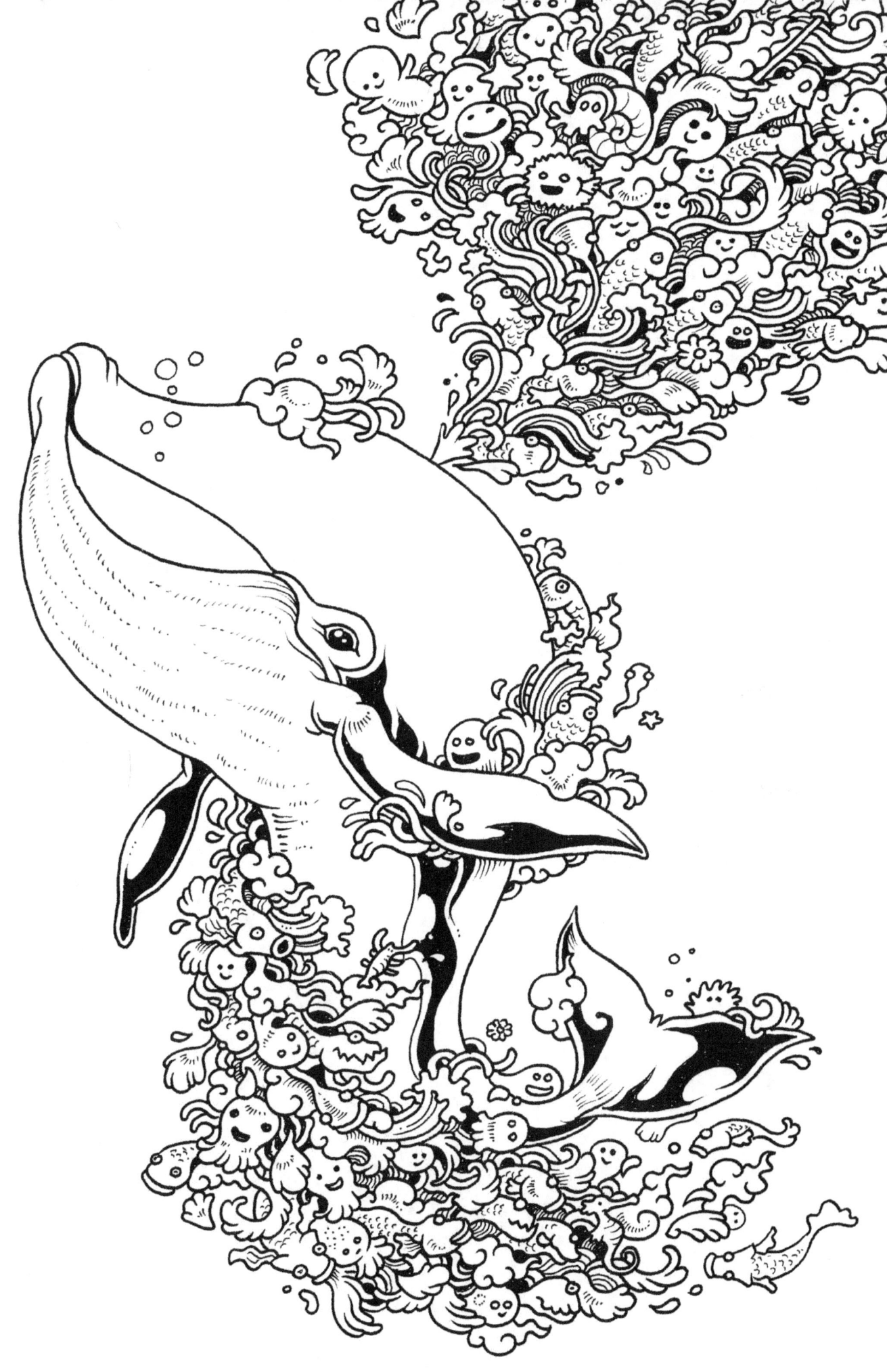

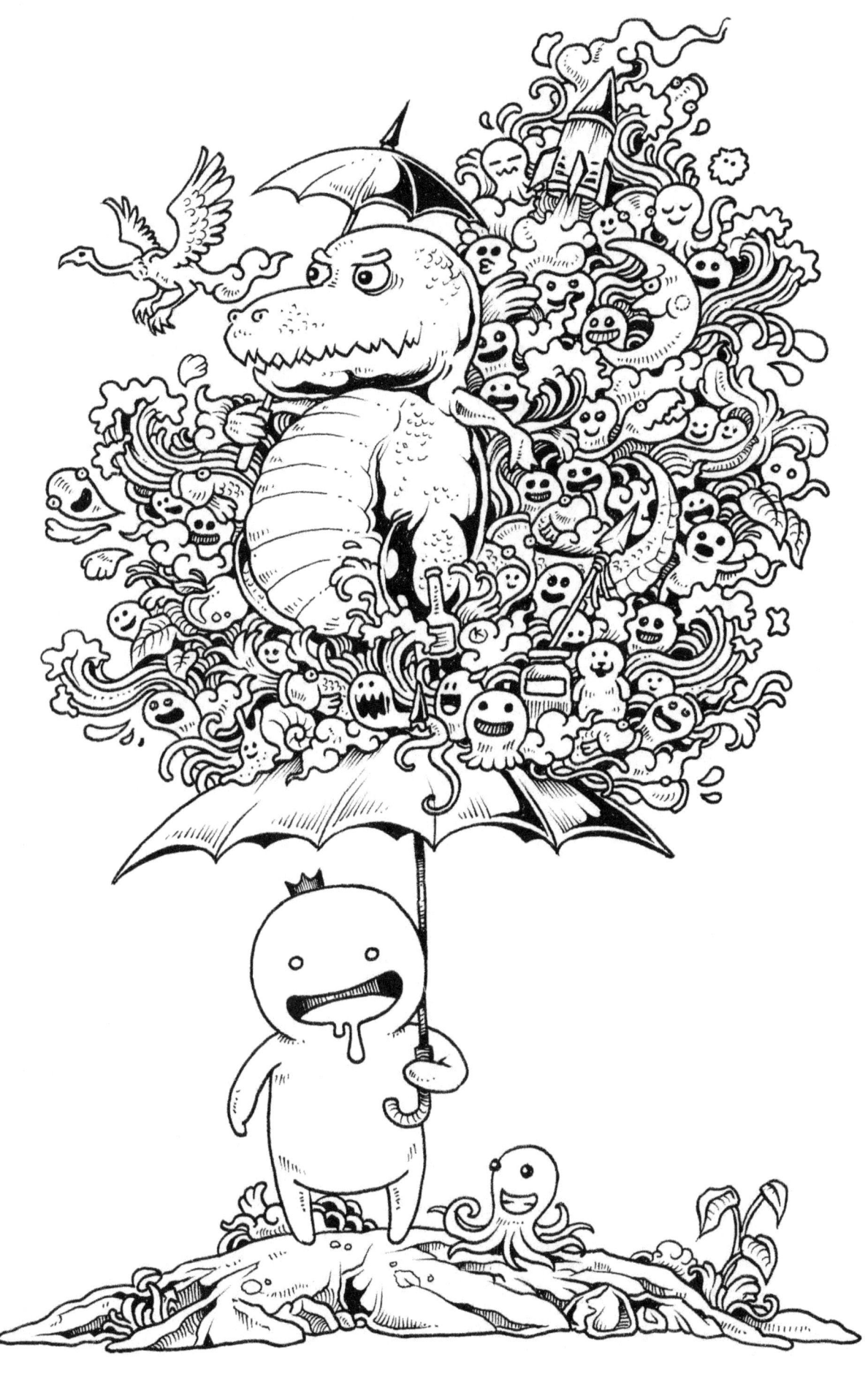

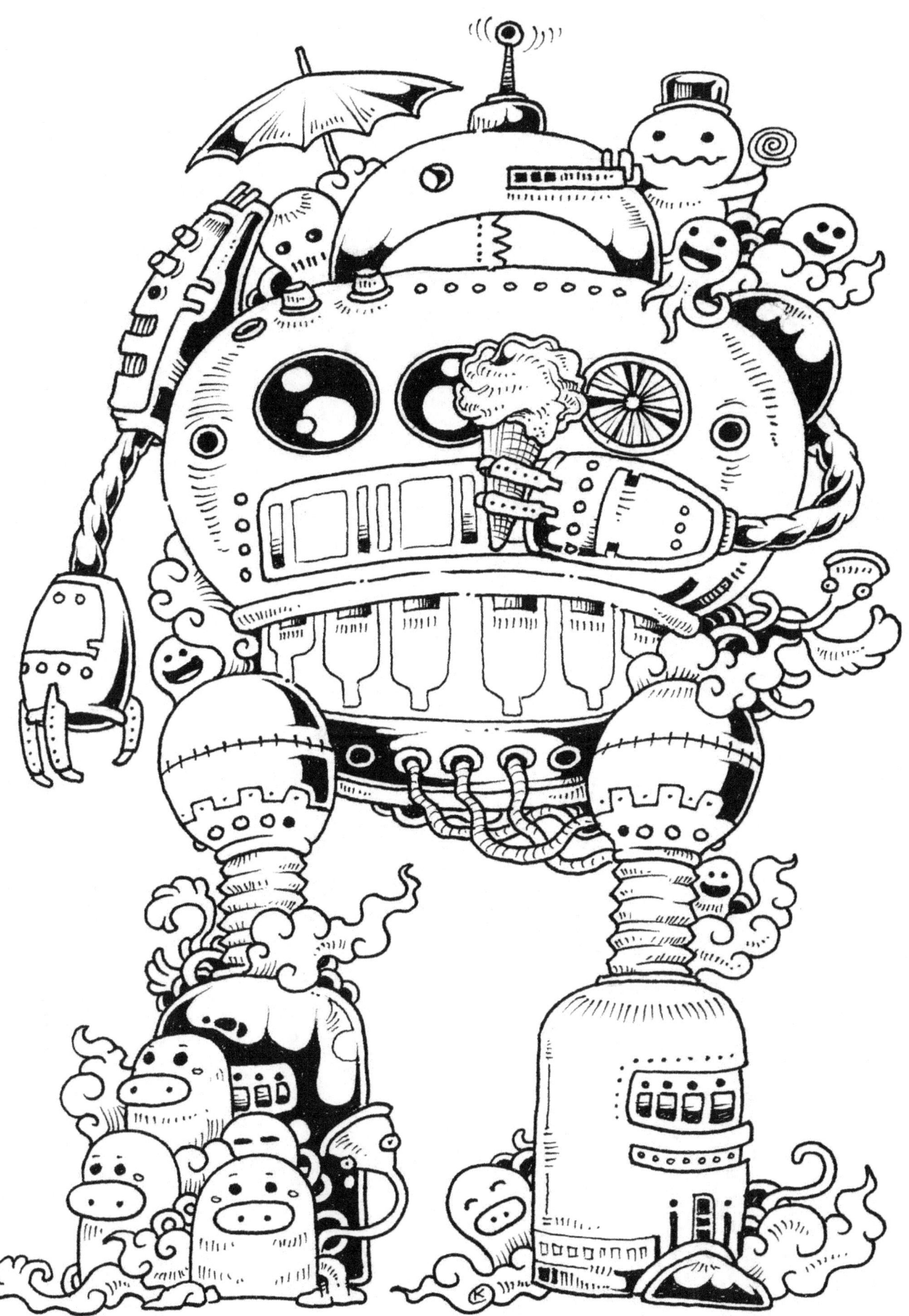

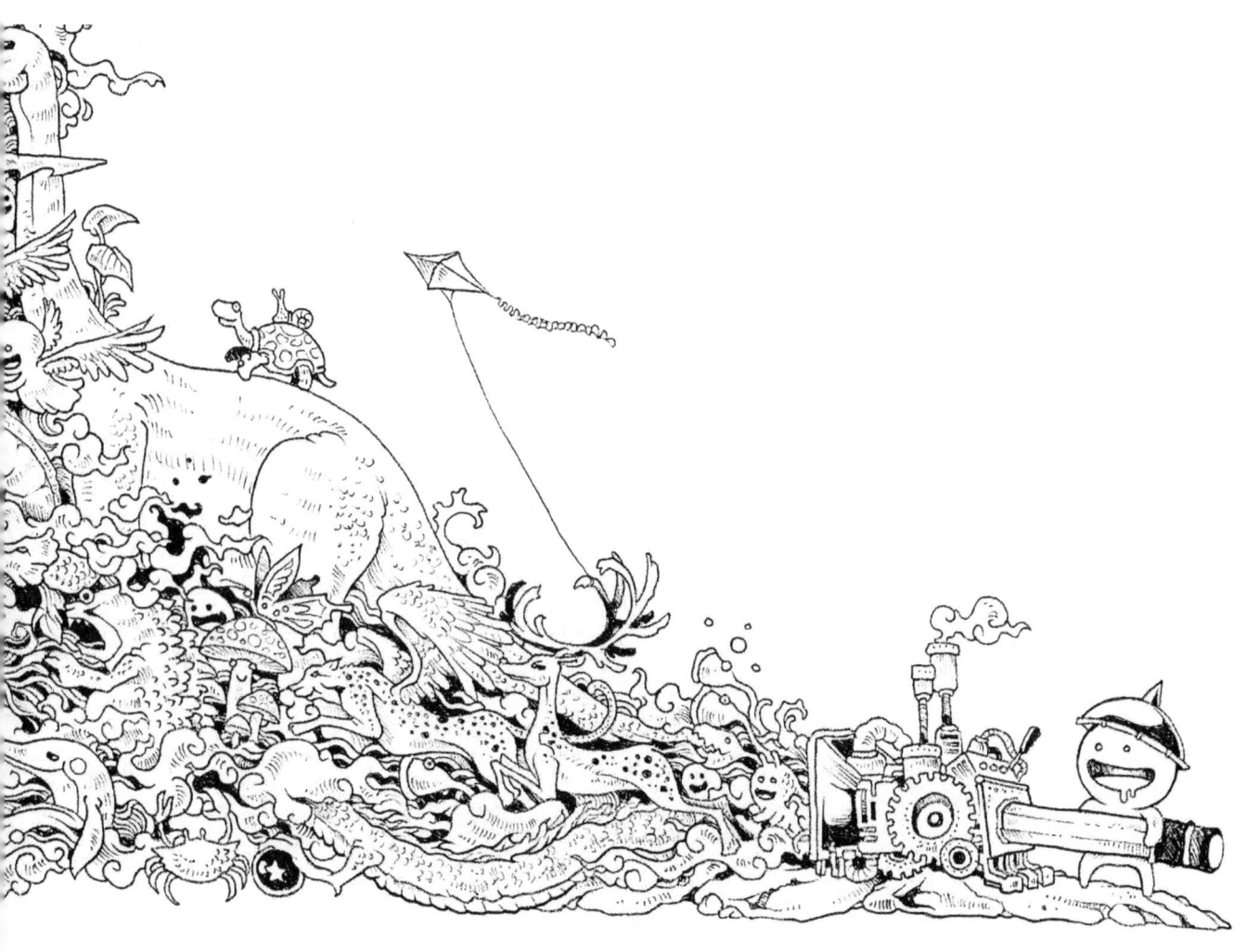

www.ingramcontent.com/pod-product-compliance
Lightning Source LLC
Chambersburg PA
CBHW080306180526

45167CB00006B/2698